SHAKESPEARE

MACBETH

IN EVERYDAY ENGLISH

COLES EDITORIAL BOARD

Bound to stay open

Publisher's Note

Otabind (Ota-bind). This book has been bound using the patented Otabind process. You can open this book at any page, gently run your finger down the spine, and the pages will lie flat.

ABOUT COLES NOTES

COLES NOTES have been an indispensible aid to students on five continents since 1948.

COLES NOTES are available for a wide range of individual literary works. Clear, concise explanations and insights are provided along with interesting interpretations and evaluations.

Proper use of COLES NOTES will allow the student to pay greater attention to lectures and spend less time taking notes. This will result in a broader understanding of the work being studied and will free the student for increased participation in discussions.

COLES NOTES are an invaluable aid for review and exam preparation as well as an invitation to explore different interpretive paths.

COLES NOTES are written by experts in their fields. It should be noted that any literary judgement expressed herein is just that – the judgement of one school of thought. Interpretations that diverge from, or totally disagree with any criticism may be equally valid.

COLES NOTES are designed to supplement the text and are not intended as a substitute for reading the text itself. Use of the NOTES will serve not only to clarify the work being studied, but should enhance the readers enjoyment of the topic.

ISBN 0-7740-3213-8

© COPYRIGHT 1997 AND PUBLISHED BY
COLES PUBLISHING COMPANY
TORONTO - CANADA
PRINTED IN CANADA

Manufactured by Webcom Limited
Cover finish: Webcom's Exclusive **DURACOAT**

CHARACTERS IN THE PLAY

Duncan: King of Scotland.

Malcolm
Donalbain } Duncan's sons.

Macbeth
Banquo
Macduff
Lennox
Ross } Noblemen of Scotland.
Menteith
Angus
Caithness

Fleance: Banquo's son.

Siward: Earl of Northumberland.

Young Siward: Siward's son.

Seyton: An officer attending on Macbeth.

Boy: Macduff's son.

A captain

An English doctor

A Scottish doctor

A porter

An old man

Three murderers

Lady Macbeth: Macbeth's wife.

Lady Macduff: Macduff's wife.

A gentlewoman: A woman attending on Lady Macbeth.

The Weird Sisters

Hecate

The ghost of Banquo

Apparitions: Various ghosts and demons.

Lords, officers, soldiers, messengers and attendants

[*Setting: Scotland and England.*

ACT I · SCENE 1

[A deserted place.]

[Thunder and lightning. Enter three witches.]

First Witch: What will be the next occasion on which we shall be gathered together again? Will it be amid the crashing of the thunderstorm, or the fierce flashes of lightning or when the rain is poured in a deluge upon the earth?

Second Witch: It will be when the confusion and turmoil are over, when the strife is ended and the result is known.

Third Witch: Then it will be soon, even before this day has vanished into night.

First Witch: Where shall we meet?

Second Witch: Upon the wild moorland.

Third Witch: We shall there see the great chief, Macbeth.

First Witch: I attend thy call, Spirit.

Second Witch: The Toad-witch summons us.

Third Witch: Immediately!

All: All good is turned to ill, and what is ill delights us, seeming good. Fly! Disappear in the murky, mist-laden air.

[Exit.]

ACT I · SCENE 2

[A camp near Forres.]

[Battle sounds. Enter Duncan, Malcolm, Donalbain and Lennox with attendants, meeting a bleeding sergeant.]

Duncan: Who is this approaching, covered with blood? Judging from his appearance, he ought to be able to give us the very latest news of the rebellion.

Malcolm: It is one of your guards, sire, who defended me bravely. If not for him I would have been made a prisoner. Welcome, my valiant helper. Tell His Majesty how the conflict stood when you left the battlefield.

Sergeant: The issue was still undecided. The two sides swayed backward and forward without either side gaining much advantage, as when two people clutch at each other in the water neither can go forward, each being held back by the other. The ruthless chief of the Macdonalds, whose evil disposition leads him naturally to be a rebel and a traitor, has a large army of Irish foot soldiers and men from the west, and seemed, at first, likely to be victorious. Fickle fortune seemed to favor his wicked designs, but her smiles were like those of a false woman, not to be trusted, and it soon appeared that Macdonald could not resist those sent against him. The valiant general, Macbeth—most worthy is he to be called valiant—cut his way, like the favored darling of the spirit of courage, through all opposition, his sword red and reeking in his hands from its deadly work. Nothing stopped him until he confronted the rebellious chief and, before he parted from him, he had cut his body in half and given his head to be exposed on our castle walls.

Duncan: My brave kinsman! A most noble man!

Sergeant: From the east, the most destructive winds and storms proceed, although it is the same point from which the lifegiving sun arises. Similarly, a new disaster did appear, immediately upon the defeat of Macdonald. Note this well, my liege. His forces had just been defeated and forced to flee from the brave men fighting for law and right, when the king of Norway, seeing a suitable opportunity, renewed the attack with fresh troops.

Duncan: Did this frighten our two brave generals?

Sergeant: They were as frightened as an eagle would be by the attack of a sparrow, or the king of beasts by that of the timid rabbit. Indeed, to tell you truly, it merely incited them to further efforts, and they fought with redoubled energy, like artillery loaded with double charges, dealing death and destruction all around. One would have thought that they intended to swim in the blood of their enemies, or to make famous another Place of Skulls. But I can say no more. My wounds overcome me.

Duncan: Thy brave words and thy injuries are both honorable to thee! Both proclaim that thou art a valiant soldier. See that his wounds are attended to.

[Exit sergeant, attended.]

Who is this approaching?

[Enter Ross.]

Malcolm: It is the noble Lord of Ross.

Lennox: The expression on his face seems to indicate sudden and important tidings.

Ross: Hail, my liege!

Duncan: Noble lord, from whence do you come?

Ross: I come from Fife, Your Majesty. There, the flags of the king of Norway, waving in the air in defiance of your power, struck a chill to the hearts of your subjects, and the king himself led on his mighty army in the attack on our troops. In this he was aided by one of your own subjects, the false and treacherous Cawdor. The fight raged on until brave Macbeth, beloved of the war goddess, faced him fully armed, and matched himself against the king. They fought hand to hand, sword opposed to sword, in deadly conflict, until Macbeth foiled and overcame the lawless invader, and the day was ours.

Duncan: This is joyful news indeed!

Ross: So that Sweno, king of Norway, now sues for terms. We refused to allow them to carry away their dead until he had paid to us a large sum of money at St. Columba's Isle.

Duncan: No longer will I look upon that traitor, Cawdor, with my former affection. He has abused my trust in him. Convey my orders that he be taken to immediate execution, and hail Macbeth as the successor to his name and estates.

Ross: Your commands shall be obeyed.

Duncan: The valiant Macbeth shall profit by Cawdor's loss.

[*Exit.*]

ACT I · SCENE 3

[*A heath near Forres.*]
[*Thunder. Enter the three witches.*]

First Witch: From whence come you, my sister?

Second Witch: I have been putting pigs to death.

Third Witch: And where hast thou been?

First Witch: I passed the wife of a sailor, sitting with a heap of chestnuts upon her knees, noisily chewing them, and I begged for some. "Be off, witch!" cried the loathsome, overfed creature. I will revenge myself for that upon her husband. He has sailed in command of a vessel to a Syrian port. I will follow after him in a leaky sieve, in the likeness of a tailless animal, and there I'll work and work, and work my vengeance upon him.

Second Witch: You shall have a favoring breeze from me.

First Witch: Many thanks, sister.

Third Witch: And from me also.

First Witch: I have all the rest in my own power, and can control the directions in which they blow, even to every point marked on the sailor's compass. This sailor shall suffer night and day. He shall wither up and dry, and his strength be drained from him. Soft, rest-giving sleep shall never more descend upon his tired eyelids, and he shall drag out his life like a man accursed. For many long, dreary weeks he shall slowly waste away, and his ship shall continuously be in the midst of storms, giving him no rest from anxiety and physical strain. Yet it shall not sink and end his misery. See what I have here.

Second Witch: Let me see, let me see.

First Witch: Here is the thumb from the hand of a pilot who was drowned on his homeward voyage.

[Drum within.]

Third Witch: I hear a drum sounding! Macbeth approaches!

All: With hands entwined, the fateful three, who travel swiftly over land and sea, circle around in the charmed dance. Three times we go in thy direction, three times in mine, and yet three times more, making up the perfect number. Hush! The enchantment is completed.

[Enter Macbeth and Banquo.]

Macbeth: I have never yet seen a day so bad in its appearance and so good in its events as this!

Banquo: Do you know how far we are from Forres? What creatures can these be here, so fantastically dressed, and so old and wrinkled? They are upon the earth, yet they are unlike any that we have seen belonging to it. Are you living beings? Are you anything that a human being may hold conversation with? By your gestures, it would seem that you comprehend what I say. You place your roughened fingers upon your thin and withered lips in a significant manner.

At first sight you appear to be women, but now I see that your chins are covered with hair, which makes me think I must be mistaken.

Macbeth: If you have the power of speech, let us hear you. Tell us what kind of beings you are.

First Witch: Greetings to thee, Macbeth, Lord of Glamis!

Second Witch: Greetings to thee, Macbeth, Lord of Cawdor!

Third Witch: Greetings to thee, Macbeth, monarch of Scotland in time to come!

Banquo: Why are you dismayed, my lord, at hearing words that predict so much good fortune? Tell me truly, ye strange appearances, are you phantoms of the imagination, or are you indeed what my eyes see before me? You have met my brave colleague with such fair words of present good fortune and future greatness that he is lost in a trance on hearing them, but you have told nothing to me. If it lies in your power to see future events in their beginnings, and you can tell which will come to pass and which will never be realized, tell something of them to me, also, though I neither ask your kindness nor dread your dislike.

First Witch: We greet thee also!

Second Witch: We greet thee!

Third Witch: Greetings to thee!

First Witch: Not so high as Macbeth, yet above him.

Second Witch: Not so fortunate, but more blessed.

Third Witch: Thy children shall reign, though thou be no monarch. Therefore, we salute thee, both Banquo and Macbeth!

First Witch: Brave generals, we hail thee both!

Macbeth: Hold. This is not enough! Explain yourselves more fully. I know that I have succeeded to the title of Glamis, but Cawdor cannot be mine, as the noble thane still holds his lands and is not in the least likely to forfeit them. Much more impossible is it to imagine that I shall ever succeed to the crown of Scotland. What is the source of your information? And why have you intercepted us on this desolate, storm-stricken moor to tell us such incredible things? Answer me, I demand of you.

[Witches vanish.]

Banquo: There are unsubstantial forms of air on the earth, I see, as well as in the water, and these strange creatures seem to be of that nature. Where have they gone?

Macbeth: Melted into the invisible air. What appeared to be a bodily form has vanished, as our breath, into the surrounding atmosphere. I wish they had remained.

Banquo: Were there really any such beings here at all? Or have we partaken unknowingly of the plant that deprives those eating it of their senses and makes them unable to judge what is real and what is not?

Macbeth: Your descendants shall reign over Scotland.

Banquo: You, yourself, shall reign over Scotland.

Macbeth: And I shall be Lord of Cawdor also—was that not what they said?

Banquo: That was exactly what they told you. Who is this?

[*Enter Ross and Angus.*]

Ross: The joyful tidings of your victory, brave general, have given great pleasure to your sovereign. Indeed, when he was told of your prowess on the battlefield, he scarcely knew which was greatest—his admiration of your gallant deeds, or the honors and applause which you deserve for the doing of them. When these considerations had left him quite unable to say more, then came the tale of your valor in the second fight against the king of Norway, and of your fearless bearing there, dealing death to all around, but refusing to fear it on your own account. The messengers followed swiftly upon each other's heels, each one having some fresh account to relate to the king of your gallant defence of his country.

Angus: He commissioned us to bear to you his royal thanks, but they are only a token of what you shall receive when we take you to him.

Ross: To show you that greater advancements await you, he commanded me to give you, in his name, the title of Lord of Cawdor. I therefore greet you by that name, which is now your own.

Banquo: Surely it cannot be that Satan has told the truth!

Macbeth: The Lord of Cawdor is not dead. While he lives, none other can hold his title. Why do you bestow upon me a name that cannot be mine?

Angus: It is true that the man who bore that title is yet living, but the short remainder of that life, which he has forfeited by his treasons, he will pass under the well-merited sentence of death. It is not known with certainty whether he actually fought in the ranks of his country's enemies, or only encouraged and aided them secretly, or whether, in both these ways, he did his utmost to bring about the downfall of his native land. What is most certain is that the most gross treachery has been proved against him, and he has admitted his horrible crime.

Macbeth: [*Aside.*] Already I am Glamis and Cawdor. Two of the three predictions fulfilled; the third and highest is yet to come. [*To Ross and Angus.*] Accept my gratitude, my lords, for your trouble. [*To Banquo.*] Do you hear how the promises of the three strange sisters to me are being quickly brought to pass? You may now safely indulge in the hope that their promise to you will also come true, and your posterity will reign over Scotland.

Banquo: If you follow up that thought and seek to complete the prophecy in its entirety, I fear it may incite you to aspire to the throne, now occupied by another, and not be content merely with the lordship of Cawdor. I admit that the coincidence is most striking, but I fear it may only be a design of evil spirits, telling us truth in things of comparatively little importance, in order that we may trust them further, when they can more easily deceive us in graver matters, and lure us to our destruction. Let me speak with you a moment, my friends.

Macbeth: [*Aside.*] Of the three predictions, two are now proved to be true. They give me joyful hope that they are but the preludes to the fulfilment of the magnificent promise that yet remains. [*To the others.*] Once more receive my thanks, my lords. [*Aside.*] I cannot tell whether to think these suggestions from the spirit world good or bad. If they are evil, why do they begin by showing themselves true? I have already received the title of Cawdor. If not evil, they would never suggest to me that terrible thought which, even to contemplate, makes my hair stand on end with terror, and my firmly placed heart, contrary to all natural use, beat furiously at the bare imagination of it. The terrors of the mind are more dreadful than immediate and tangible dangers. That dread thought, which is only a phantom in my brain, has such power over my whole being that it almost deprives my faculties of their customary use. They are lost in overwhelming amazement and conjecture, and have no power any longer to discriminate between the real and the unreal.

Banquo: See! Our companion is completely absorbed in thought!

Macbeth: [*Aside.*] If it be my destiny to be crowned king of Scotland, then my destiny must work itself out without my aid. I am resolved to remain passive.

Banquo: The assuming of new titles and dignities is like the putting on of new clothes. One requires a little time to become accustomed to them.

Macbeth: [*Aside.*] Well, let happen what may, all will end at last. The moments fly quickly through whatever troubles they lead us.

Banquo: Noble general, we await your convenience.

Macbeth: I crave your forgiveness. My slow mind was occupied in recalling past events. Good friends, your kindness is written in my heart, where I may be continually reminded of it. Come, we will go to His Majesty. [*Aside to Banquo.*] Ponder well what has just occurred and, later, when we have well considered it, we will open our minds to each other frankly on this subject.

Banquo: Most willingly.

Macbeth: Say no more at present. Let us go, my lords.

[*Exit.*]

ACT I · SCENE 4

[*Forres: The palace.*]
[*Flourish of trumpets. Enter Duncan, Malcolm,
Donalbain, Lennox and attendants.*]

Duncan: Has the sentence been carried out that was pronounced on the rebellious thane? Have they come back yet, who were appointed to see it done?

Malcolm: They have not yet returned, Your Majesty. But I have seen one who was present at Cawdor's execution, and he tells me that the thane never showed himself to such advantage in all his life before, as he did at the moment of quitting this world. He freely admitted that he had offended deeply against his country and his sovereign, and begged forgiveness of Your Majesty, saying that he sorrowed sincerely for his fault. He carried himself like one who wished to make it plain that he held his life lightly and, though it was his most precious possession, yet he could part with it as easily as if it were the smallest thing he owned.

Duncan: I see that a person's thoughts and character cannot be judged very well by any indications in the face. I placed the most implicit confidence in the thane of Cawdor.

[*Enter Macbeth, Banquo, Ross and Angus.*]

My noble kinsman! I was recently lamenting that I could never repay thy invaluable services to me. Thou hast accomplished so much that no rewards or honors can ever equal thy deservings. I could even wish that thou had done less, so that my gratitude and the rewards which I can bestow upon thee might bear at least an approximate relation to thy gallant deeds. But I can only tell thee that I owe thee more than I can adequately repay.

Macbeth: In the rendering of my knightly duty and loyalty to my lord, I am amply rewarded. It is the role of a king to receive service from his followers. They are merely fulfilling their bound duty to their king and country when they perform these services, as sons of their country and liegemen to their sovereign, honorably safeguarding both the one and the other.

Duncan: I am glad to see thee here. I have taken the first steps toward thy advancement, and it shall be my constant care to see that thou continuest to flourish. Gallant Banquo, thy achievements are equally great, and it shall be known that they are so. Come, let me embrace thee, close to this heart, which beats with gratitude to thee.

Banquo: If I be planted in that royal heart, all that is mine in life and deed is at your service.

Duncan: My heart is so full of gladness that it overflows at my eyes, counterfeiting the signs of mourning. My children, cousins and lords, and you, my kinsmen, who stand in near proximity to the throne, hear us announce that we do now declare the eldest prince, Malcolm, the heir to the crown and kingdom. Therefore, we bestow upon him the title of the heir—Prince of Cumberland. And, we also declare that not only the prince shall be invested with a title, but all those whose deeds merit it shall receive a similar reward. Let us now leave this place and set forth for Inverness, and place ourselves under still further obligations to our brave general.

Macbeth: The time that is unemployed in your service is no rest, but is more wearing than any arduous task. I will take upon myself the pleasant duty of being your forerunner and convey to my wife the glad tidings of your visit. I respectfully bid Your Majesty adieu.

Duncan: Noble thane!

Macbeth: [*Aside.*] He is Prince of Cumberland—the heir! I must arrange some plan to overcome him, or he will cause my downfall. He stands in the way of my ambition, and must be removed. Ye lights of the firmament, quench your flames. My wishes are too deadly and terrible for anything but darkness. Let the eye close itself to what the hand would perform, yet let it be performed, even that terrible deed which the eye dares not look upon.   [*Exit.*]

Duncan: You say well, good Banquo. Macbeth is indeed as gallant a man as you tell me. I love to hear his praises. I feast upon the recital of his prowess, and rejoice in it. He has gone in advance to prepare for us. Let us follow him now, my noble cousin!

[*Flourish of trumpets. All exit.*]

ACT I · SCENE 5
[*Inverness. Macbeth's castle.*]
[*Enter Lady Macbeth, reading a letter.*]

Lady Macbeth: "These strange creatures greeted me immediately after I had been victorious in battle. I have, since then, made diligent inquiry concerning them, and I find that they are confidently supposed to be possessed of a supernatural wisdom. I wished, earnestly, to ask them more than they told, but, as I was questioning them, they suddenly vanished from sight. I stood lost in amazement. Before I had recovered myself, messengers came from King Duncan, and saluted me by one of the titles that the witches had promised me. They had also promised that in the future I should reign over Scotland. My dear wife, and sharer of my fortunes, I am informing thee of these matters as quickly as possible, in order that thou may rejoice with me in knowing what good fortune is in store for thee. Take these words to thy bosom, and ponder them well. Adieu."

My husband, thou art already Thane of Glamis and Thane of Cawdor. Have no fear but that thou shalt also be king. The one thing that may hold thee back is thine own kind-hearted disposition, which I fear will prevent thee from achieving thy ambition in the quickest way. Thou hast the will and the desire to rise, but hast not the evil nature which would cast aside all scruples in order to attain its object. Thou would soar above thy fellows, but would not commit sin in order to do so. Thou would not refuse to enjoy the results of a crime, provided thou wert not called upon to perform it. Thy desires center upon the throne and, if thou art indeed to have it, the way is plain. The deed calls aloud that which must be done before thou can grasp the crown. O, hasten to me, that I may incite thee to prompt and fearless action, that I may infuse my vigor into thy mind and, by my burning words, dissipate all the doubts and scruples which hold thee back from grasping at that summit of earthly ambition, a kingly crown, which thou art fated both by the supernatural powers and by destiny to obtain. What news do you bring?

[*Enter a messenger.*]

Messenger: King Duncan will this night be your guest.

Lady Macbeth: You must be insane to tell me this! Had it been so, we would have been told of it by your lord, who accompanies the king, so that we might be in readiness to receive His Majesty.

Messenger: Indeed, madam, it is so. My lord is even now on his way, but one of his men outpaced him, and reached here first. The man is almost spent, and could only with difficulty deliver his news.

Lady Macbeth: See that he is cared for. His message is of the highest importance.

[*Exit messenger.*]

The very voice fails and falters that heralds the coming of the king to this castle, where his doom awaits him. Surround me now, you evil ones, that suggest to our minds the deadly thoughts of crime. Make me forget my womanhood, harden my heart, prevent the natural flow of my blood and pour into my whole being the most relentless inhumanity. Let my breast be untouched by all influence of gentle pity, and let no remorseful prickings of conscience have any effect upon my stern design, or come between the intention and the performance.

Replace the natural, womanly feelings of my bosom with bitterness and hate, you servants and helpers of all wickedness, wherever you dwell, invisible to mortal eye. Darkness, approach and cover thyself in the deeper darkness of Erebus until thou hide the deed that is to be done, even from the murderous instrument that shall perform it.

Let no light pierce the black covering of night to discover and frustrate our fatal purpose.

[*Enter Macbeth.*]

Hail, high chieftain! Glamis and Cawdor both! And I greet thee by a yet higher title than either, according to the promise for thy future. My mind has flown to that happy future, carried there by the joyful news contained in thy letter. I enjoy already, in anticipation, the glories of that great destiny.

Macbeth: Beloved wife, the king is on his way here, and will lodge with us this night.

Lady Macbeth: How long does he plan to remain?

Macbeth: Only until tomorrow.

Lady Macbeth: Never shall any tomorrow witness the departure of Duncan from this castle.

My husband, you show plainly on your face that unusual thoughts are filling your breast. Do not display your innermost feelings to all the world. Deceive the world. Put on a face suitable for the occasion. Be ready to give a joyful greeting to your sovereign when he arrives, undimmed by any secret thoughts of fear. Show a face as seemingly innocent as the summer blossoms, though your thoughts be deadly as the poisonous snake. There is much to arrange for our visitor. And, as for what we intend to accomplish this night, I will be responsible for that. We shall then secure for all the rest of our lives the advantages of kingly rule and power, which the carrying out of that purpose will give to us.

Macbeth: We will talk of this again, later.

Lady Macbeth: Remember to meet the king with a frank and open expression. Show no evidence on your features of your hidden purpose. It is the sign of a weak mind to be unable to keep a steadfast face. Have no care for the details of our plan: I will arrange all.

[*Exit.*]

ACT I · SCENE 6

[*In front of Macbeth's castle.*]
[*Oboe music and torches flaring. Enter Duncan, Malcolm, Donalbain, Banquo, Lennox, Macduff, Ross, Angus and attendants.*]

Duncan: This mansion of Macbeth's is delightfully situated, and the fresh balmy air greets our senses most refreshingly.

Banquo: The swallows, loved favorites of all, who visit us in the warmest season of the year, show by the numbers of their tiny dwellings clustered around the castle that the air is sweet and delicate here. There does not seem to be a single projection or line of wall, not a supporting pillar or a convenient corner, that these little martins have not taken possession of, and there hung their nests and reared their tiny broods. I have often noticed that in the favorite nesting places of these little summer visitants the air is fragrant and pure.

[*Enter Lady Macbeth.*]

Duncan: Look! Our kind Lady Macbeth, whose guests we are to be, comes to give us welcome. Sometimes, dear lady, our friends' mode of showing their affection for us may cause us some inconvenience, but we gladly suffer that inconvenience for the affection's sake. I hope that you will so regard it in this case. Our royal visit to you, I fear, puts you to some trouble, but it springs from our affection and loving regard for you and your noble lord. Therefore, I trust that you will look upon it in that light, and take this manifestation of our regard as some slight compensation.

Lady Macbeth: Your Majesty, if we did all that we have done, and then repeated every service again and again, it would still bear very poor comparison with the overwhelming proofs of kindness and the ample rewards which Your Majesty has bestowed upon us. We offer you our most heartfelt thanks, both for your former benefits and more recent honors, for which we are ever Your Majesty's humble servants, remembering you continually in our prayers.

Duncan: Is not the gallant chieftain himself here? We followed him swiftly, and intended to arrive before him. But his keen affections, aided by his splendid horsemanship, have carried him to your side in less time than we could accomplish the journey. Honored lady, we will lodge with you this night.

Lady Macbeth: Welcome, my king, to all that we have or hold. Your faithful subjects are, at all times, ready to render to their sovereign what is really his own, and is held in trust for him.

Duncan: Let me take your hand, and you will lead me to your husband, for whom we have a great affection and esteem. Our royal favor shall long continue to be extended to him. Allow me, dear lady.

[*Exit.*]

ACT I · SCENE 7

[*Macbeth's castle.*]
[*Oboe music and flaring torches. Enter several servants with dishes and glasses, who then pass over the stage. Then enter Macbeth.*]

Macbeth: If this business were entirely finished with, when once the deed has been committed, then it would be best to get it over as promptly as possible. If only the one murderous blow were all that need be considered. If, then, no further results continued to flow from the deed and the whole affair would be ended, and ensure the satisfactory attainment of our object, even here in this short period of mortal life, upon this narrow shore of the boundless ocean of eternity, then we would willingly take the risk of punishment in a future world. But, in an instance of this kind, the punishment falls upon us while we yet live. All that we accomplish is to show an example of evil, which is speedily turned against ourselves. The equity of heaven turns the very means we have used against others into the instruments of our own ruin. There are many and weighty reasons against committing this deed.

The king has implicit confidence in me. He trusts to my honor, both as a near relation and a faithful subject. The sacred laws of hospitality ought to urge me to defend his life to the utmost while he is within my gates, rather than be the one to commit so dastardly an outrage upon him. Another consideration to withhold me from it is the king's own personal character. His life has been so gentle, so frank, open and irreproachable, so utterly void of offence to his people, that there is neither the excuse of arrogance, nor of false and underhanded dealings to cause me to raise my hand against him, or for others to applaud the deed. The remembrance of these good qualities in the murdered sovereign will be his strongest advocate and the most powerful condemnation of those who commit the foul crime. The invisible winds themselves, as if ridden by the sweet spirit of compassion, or by the angelic messengers of heaven, will spread the dreadful tidings over all the land, until tears of grief and universal mourning shall descend like rain.

There is not a single motive to urge me to the deed, excepting love of power, which often leads those who aspire to its soaring heights to overshoot their mark and bring about their own speedy downfall.

[*Enter Lady Macbeth.*]

Do you bring tidings, dear lady?

Lady Macbeth: The king has almost finished his meal. You ought not to have left his presence.

Macbeth: Did he notice that I had gone?

Lady Macbeth: Indeed he did.

Macbeth: Listen, dear lady. Let us give up our plans and take no further steps toward this ambitious project we have discussed together. The king has shown himself most favorably disposed toward me, and has heaped benefits upon me. My recent victories have won me the applause and admiration of all ranks. We should enjoy these advantages now to the full, while they show so fair. If we carry out our plans, we must say farewell to all these pleasant experiences.

Lady Macbeth: Then has the intoxication of delightful anticipation, which filled you when you first spoke to me of this, entirely passed away? Are those feelings now drowned in slumber? Or are they awaking in terror at their former exuberance and looking in fear and dread at what they were, then, perfectly ready to carry out? After this, I shall value thy affection for me as being of the same transitory nature. Dost thou indeed shrink from doing what thou dost not shrink from wishing? Thou desirest the crown, as the most precious thing this world has to bestow, and yet thou are willing to confess thyself afraid to do what is necessary to obtain it, like the miserable cat, which the proverb tells us, "would eat fish, but would not wet her feet."

Macbeth: Say no more. This is not a question of ordinary courage. It is a question of manhood, of right and wrong.

My courage is equal to any demand that may rightfully be made upon a man. He who oversteps that bound ceases to be one, and becomes a mere destroying animal.

Lady Macbeth: Then is that what you were when you first told me of this? Your own words condemn you. It was you who first introduced the subject. You were not then afraid, and you will scarcely admit that you had become a beast! If now your daring rises to a higher pitch, you will be greater than before, and not less. You had no idea then that there would ever be a suitable opportunity to achieve your ends, yet you ardently wished for one, and would always have endeavored to create it. Now, the opportunity is placed in your hands, and it causes your resolution to give way. I have nursed my babes, and know the loving solicitude of a mother for her child, and yet I could have steeled my heart against its friendly smiles, taken the life-giving drink from its childish mouth and nerved myself to cast it to destruction, if I had given my word to do so, as you vowed to do this.

Macbeth: But what if we should not succeed?

Lady Macbeth: Not succeed! If you will only raise your daring to the necessary height and not let it fall again from there, we must succeed. The king will be weary with his tiresome hours of travel, and will undoubtedly sleep heavily. When he has retired, I will ply the men appointed to guard his room with strong drink until it overcomes them, and remembrance, which warns the intellect of what it has to fear, shall fail in its duty and become a mere cloudy vapor, and the brain shall be stupefied, its powers drawn from it, as in a still. Then, the defenceless king will lie exposed to whatever we may do, while those are lying in drunken slumber who should guard his life. We can then give any explanation we choose. His wine-drenched servants will not be able to clear themselves if we throw upon them the blame of our tremendous crime.

Macbeth: Thou should bear none but sons. Thy strong and fearless nature should never give birth to tender maids. Do you think that if we use the weapons of the guards to commit the deed and then smear the men with blood, people will believe they are the murderers?

Lady Macbeth: No one will be bold enough to suggest other-

16

wise. And we must be foremost and loudest in lamenting Duncan's death.

Macbeth: I have definitely taken my resolution. Now, I will steel every sinew and strain every nerve for the accomplishment of my dreadful task. Let us go, and deceive everyone, in the meantime, with the appearance of friendliness and ease. Our faces must be masks, showing a counterfeit appearance and concealing the hollowness beneath.

[Exit.]

ACT II · SCENE 1

[Court of Macbeth's castle.]

[Enter Banquo, and Fleance bearing a torch.]

Banquo: What is the hour, my son?

Fleance: It is past the setting of the moon, but I have not heard the hour strike.

Banquo: The moon sets at midnight.

Fleance: I think it is past that hour, my lord.

Banquo: Wait a moment. Here, hold my weapon. They are practising economy above, and showing no lights. Carry this also. I am very weary. My eyes are weighed down with sleep, but I dare not give way to it. O ye heavenly spirits, do not allow the evil thoughts to gain the mastery over me, which crowd upon me when my will is laid to rest in sleep.

[Enter Macbeth, and a servant with a torch.]

Hand me my weapon again. Who comes here?

Macbeth: No enemy.

Banquo: You, my lord! Have you not yet gone to bed? The king is sleeping. He has been greatly delighted by his reception, and has bestowed generous gifts upon your servants. He sends this diamond to Lady Macbeth, calling her his most loving entertainer, and he is completely filled with a blissful satisfaction.

Macbeth: We would willingly have served him better but, as we had so little notice of his visit, we were obliged to do as well as we could under the circumstances, though not as well as we could have wished, had we had free scope for our desires.

Banquo: The king is quite satisfied as it is. The three witches visited me last night in my dreams. Their predictions to you seem to have been very accurate.

Macbeth: I have never thought any more about them. But I would like to talk the subject over with you once more when we have time to do so, if you would be good enough to spare me an hour.

Banquo: I will await your gracious convenience.

Macbeth: Should it ever come true, and you remain faithful to me, you shall be most highly advanced.

Banquo: I shall gladly be guided by you, provided that in seeking to add to my honors I do not forfeit my honor, but may still be faithful to you in all frankness and sincerity.

18

Macbeth: Meanwhile, may you rest well.

Banquo: I thank you, my lord, and wish the same on your behalf.

[*Exit Banquo and Fleance.*]

Macbeth: Go to Lady Macbeth, and ask her to sound the bell when my night cup is prepared. And then you may go to rest.

[*Exit servant.*]

What is this that appears before my eyes? A weapon, as if it were offering itself to my grasp. I will seize it. My grasp encloses nothing, and yet it floats before me still. Thou deadly apparition, can thou not be felt, as well as seen? Art thou only an illusion of the brain, a phantom, produced by my overwrought mind? Thou art still present, as plainly visible as this steel, which now I pluck from its scabbard, pointing in the direction which I was about to take, when I would have used just such a dagger as thou appearest to be.

The strain on my senses has brought them to such a pitch that they produce deceiving visions to my eyes. But, if my eyes see truly, and thou art real, then are they the only senses worth trusting. Still thou art hovering before me, and now thy handle and keen blade are smeared and clotted with blood. Thou did not appear thus at first. It cannot be real. This is merely a hallucination of the mind, over-strained with dwelling on my murderous task. Now lies this hemisphere in sleep and darkness, as if drained of life. Evil thoughts hold power over men's minds as they lie slumbering. Now the infernal rites of magic are paid to Hecate, pale goddess of the dead. Sudden and violent death, gaunt and ghostly, hears the long-drawn howl of the night-roving wolf and, taking it as his signal, glides along with sinuous movements, like the cursed Tarquin, bent on evil. With silent steps he creeps like a ghost toward his victim. Be my footsteps inaudible to thee, thou solid ground beneath my feet. Tell not of my direction, nor voice my deeds. Let not a sound re-echo from thee to disturb this deathly silence, a fitting shroud for the awful deed about to be enacted. But he is still living, while I am wasting my breath in empty menaces. Too many words will allow time for the fire of my intention to die out. [*A bell rings.*] Hark! The signal sounds. Be deaf to its tones, O king. It rings thy doom, and is the signal for thy entrance into another world, of bliss or woe!

[Exit]

ACT II · SCENE 2

[*Macbeth's castle.*]
[*Enter Lady Macbeth.*]

Lady Macbeth: The wine, which has overcome their senses, has exhilarated mine. I could now face any danger. Hush! Listen! It was but the hoot of the owl, with his solemn farewell today. Macbeth is doing the deed now. I left the access to the king's chamber open, and the drunken guards sleeping heavily. I mixed narcotics with their spiced wine, so that they are now almost insensible. One can scarcely tell whether they are dead or alive.

Macbeth: [*Within.*] Ho, there! Who is that?

Lady Macbeth: Oh me! The men must have awakened and prevented him from accomplishing his purpose. We have lost all for nothing. We are discovered without having reaped any benefit from our crime. Listen, again! I saw that their knives were laid where he could find them easily. If Duncan had not reminded me so strongly of my loved parent in his sleep, I could have done it myself.

[*Enter Macbeth.*]

My brave lord!

Macbeth: It is accomplished. Did thou hear anything?

Lady Macbeth: Yes. I heard the hoot of the owl, and the chirp of the cricket. But you spoke, did you not?

Macbeth: At what time?

Lady Macbeth: A moment ago.

Macbeth: As I was coming down?

Lady Macbeth: Yes.

Macbeth: Listen! Who sleeps in the room next to the king's?

Lady Macbeth: His younger son.

Macbeth: These hands are a sad spectacle.

[*Looking on his hands.*]

Lady Macbeth: It is nonsense to say that.

Macbeth: I heard one man laugh, as he lay sleeping. Another was restless and cried out in alarm. They roused each other by their noise, while I stood listening. Then I heard them repeat their prayers and settle themselves to slumber again.

Lady Macbeth: Yes. Two are sleeping in the same chamber.

Macbeth: One asked God's blessing upon them, and the other replied "amen," as if they had known what I was doing, and the sight of my hands, covered with the dreadful witness of guilt, had terrified them. I tried to say "amen" too, but it was impossible.

Lady Macbeth: You must not take it so seriously to heart.

Macbeth: Why was it that I was unable to echo that "amen"? My voice refused to utter the word, though I much desired the benediction.

Lady Macbeth: We dare not allow ourselves to dwell upon what we have done in this manner. If we do, we shall realize what it means, and it will deprive us of our senses.

Macbeth: It seemed to me that I heard these words: "Awake! Slumber not! Macbeth hath killed restful slumber." Soft slumber, in which all are equally harmless for a time, alike the guilty criminal and the innocent babe. Sweet rest, that winds up for us all the tangled webs of our daily cares and anxieties, and straightens it out again, in which each day sinks down to deep repose, as our lives sink to rest in the grave. Sleep, that soothes and refreshes the toilworn and weary, that heals the stings and smarts of our wounded spirits, and comes as a thankful relief, wisely provided by our mother, nature, after our hours of toil, and restores and builds up our strength for further struggle more effectively than anything else we know—

Lady Macbeth: What are you talking of?

Macbeth: Still those tones rang through the air: "Awake! Slumber not! Never more shall repose be known in this house, where it has been so foully destroyed. Never more shall Macbeth know repose!"

Lady Macbeth: Do you imagine that it was a real voice, calling to you? My dear lord, these wild imaginary fears are unworthy of you. They are beneath your customary firmness of mind. Wash your hands and cleanse them of those hideous telltale stains. You ought to have left these weapons in the king's chamber—they must be found there. Take them back and mark the drowsy guards with stains of blood.

Macbeth: Never. I can scarcely command myself even to think of the deed I have just committed, much less to go back again into the very presence of it, and see it before me.

Lady Macbeth: Weak and irresolute! I will take them myself. None but children are afraid of the picture of a terror, and those wrapped in sleep and death are no more than mere images, or lifeless representations of themselves. Should there be much blood, I will redden the faces of the guards with it, for it must appear that they are the criminals.

[*Exit. Knocking within.*]

Macbeth: Where does that noise of hammering come from? What a condition I must be in, when I jump in terror at the slightest sound! O these bloodstained hands! They almost blast my sight. Will they ever be cleansed, even by the waters of all the world, under the rule of the mighty sea god? Never can I hope to free them from these murderous stains. Sooner will they turn the dark green seas to uniform crimson.

[*Re-enter Lady Macbeth.*]

Lady Macbeth: See, I now have hands as red as your own, but I would scorn to show the same timidity of heart. [*Knocking within.*] Someone is seeking admittance at the southern gate. Let us go to our room and free ourselves from these witnesses to our guilt. It can be done without difficulty by the aid of a little water. Your firmness appears to have entirely deserted you. [*Knocking within.*] Come, my lord, they are knocking again. We must have on our night robes, in case anyone requires us. We must not be found awake and fully dressed. Do not be overcome by your thoughts in so mean and cowardly a manner.

Macbeth: In seeking to rouse me from my thoughts, you remind me of my deed. And then I wish I were not conscious that I am myself, that I am the one who has just perpetrated it. [*Knocking within.*] O could they but arouse the king by their clamor! How devoutly do I wish it were possible!

[*Exit.*]

ACT II · SCENE 3

[*The same.*]
[*Knocking within. Enter a porter.*]

Porter: What a battering and beating at the gate! Whoever is in charge of the entrance to Hades will have a rare time locking and unlocking. [*Knocking within.*] Batter, batter! Who are you, in the devil's name? Here comes a farmer who committed suicide because he feared corn was about to become cheap and plentiful, and so he would lose his profits. You come at a convenient time, farmer. Have you a good supply of handkerchiefs with you? You will need them all when you work in this heat. [*Knocking within.*] Hammer, hammer! Who comes next, in the name of Satan? A quibbler, skilled in using ambiguous words. He could seem to agree with both sides and take part with neither. He shuffled and quibbled all his life long, doing incalculable harm, and making it appear to be done in the name of heaven. But, when he came to die, his shiftiness gained him nothing then. Welcome here, quibbler. [*Knocking within.*] Beat, beat, beat! Whom have we this time? Here comes a Saxon, a maker of clothes, sent here for theft. He was making garments in the French fashion, and stole some of the material. Enter here, tailor. You will find this a good place in which to heat your iron. [*Knocking within.*] Still more knocking! Shall I never be left in peace! Who is it now! But I'll pretend no longer to be porter at Hades' gate. This place is not hot enough to keep up the idea. I intended to admit many more of the callings in which men find themselves travelling easily to ruin along the path of pleasure. But I will attend to my proper duties. [*Knocking within.*] Yes, yes, immediately! Please do not forget the gatekeeper.

[*Opens the gate.*]
[*Enter Macduff and Lennox.*]

Macduff: You did not go to rest very early, my good fellow, or you would have been awake before this.

Porter: Indeed, my lord, we were feasting and drinking until about three o'clock, for the cock had crowed for the second time.

Macduff: Is thy lord awake yet?

[*Enter Macbeth.*]

Ah! Here he comes. We have aroused him with our clamor at the gate.

Lennox: Good morning, worthy chieftain.

Macbeth: Good morning to you, and you, my Lord Macduff.

Macduff: Has the king risen yet, my good lord?

Macbeth: He is not yet awake.

Macduff: He told me to come to him early this morning. I have barely arrived at the appointed time.

Macbeth: I will take you to his chamber.

Macduff: I fear I trouble you, but I know you do it gladly.

Macbeth: When we have a congenial task to perform, the pleasure we take in its performance neutralizes any trouble or inconvenience we may experience. Here is the king's room.

Macduff: I will take the liberty of rousing him, for so he appointed me to do.

[Exit.]

Lennox: Does His Majesty depart today?

Macbeth: Yes. He gave orders to that effect.

Lennox: What a wild night it has been! The wind brought down the chimneys of the house where we lodged. People say that they heard dismal wailings and terrible shrieks through the night, seeming, in awe-inspiring tones, to predict dreadful conflagrations and catastrophes about to fall upon the world. The owl, too, hooted dismally the whole night through. And there was a report that the solid ground trembled, as in a fit.

Macbeth: Truly, it was a terrible night.

Lennox: I cannot remember in my short life ever having experienced one like it.

[Re-enter Macduff.]

Macduff: O dread and terror! O awful sight, beyond all thought or expression!

Macbeth:
Lennox: } What has happened?

Macduff: Ruin has now achieved its most fearful work—it can go no farther. Wicked hands have destroyed the sacred body of heaven's anointed king, and the spirit has fled.

Macbeth: What do I hear? The spirit fled?

Lennox: You cannot mean the king!

Macduff: Go to the room yourselves, and there behold a spectacle to turn you into stone with horror, as by Medusa's head. Do not ask me to tell you. Look for yourselves, then you will cry out too.

[Exit Macbeth and Lennox.]

Arise! Awaken, all! Rouse yourselves! Sound the alarm! Treachery! Villainy! Murder! Awake, Banquo! Awake, sons of Duncan! Rouse yourselves from drowsy slumber, which seems too much like death. Awake, and behold death in reality. Come, and look at the picture of the judgment day itself. Banquo and Malcolm, rise from sleep as ghosts risen from the tomb, to be in keeping with this awful scene. Sound the alarm!

[Bell rings.]
[Enter Lady Macbeth.]

Lady Macbeth: Some terrible thing must have happened, that such fearful sounds alarm the house and summon us from our sleep. What is it? Tell me.

Macduff: O my dear lady, the news I have to tell is too dreadful for you to listen to! The mere recital of it would kill a tender woman.

[Enter Banquo.]

O Banquo, noble friend, our dear sovereign is killed!

Lady Macbeth: Ah, misery! Can that be true? And within our gates!

Banquo: A villainous deed, wherever done. My dear friend, tell me you are mistaken, and this dreadful thing has not happened.

[Re-enter Macbeth and Lennox.]

Macbeth: How happy would I have been, had I left the world before this happened! I would have lived quite long enough, and seen the best of my days. Now all that is highest and most worthy in this mortal life has gone; nothing remains but vanity. Fair fame and kindly favor are lost to us; the flavor of life has been taken way and the insipid dregs are all that we can now boast of beneath the skies.

[Enter Malcolm and Donalbain.]

Donalbain: What is wrong?

Macbeth: Yourself. Trouble has fallen upon you, and you are still in ignorance of it. The fountain from which you drew your life no longer flows. The very wellspring of your being is dried up.

Macduff: The king, your father, has been killed.

Malcolm: Oh! Who has done this?

Lennox: It appears to have been his own attendants, for they were found with bloodstains upon their cheeks and hands. Their weapons, which were lying by them, were wet with blood. When we went in, they gazed at us in a wild and dazed manner. No one was safe in their company.

Macbeth: Nevertheless, I am sorry that I slew them in my sudden rage.

Macduff: Why did you do that?

Macbeth: You cannot expect any man to reason temperately under the influence of such conflicting emotions as overcame us on seeing the murdered king. Can one be overwhelmed with a shock of surprise, fiercely wrathful and lovingly faithful and, at the same time, show thoughtful wisdom, restrained feelings and a determination to remain passive in the face of events? The thing is impossible.

My feelings of affection and loyalty to my murdered sovereign carried me into action before calm deliberation could bid me to control myself. On the one side lay the king, the crimson stains marking his fair white body, and the gaping wounds showing like a broken defence through which destruction had entered. On the other, the guilty pair, the signs of their evil deed all over them, and their weapons steeped to the hilt in blood. Could anyone who had the least spark of affection for his murdered monarch, and valor enough to show it, restrain the impulse to avenge his king?

Lady Macbeth: Assist me from the room, I pray.

Macduff: See that Lady Macbeth is attended to.

Malcolm: [*Aside to Donalbain.*] Why are we saying nothing, when this concerns us more nearly than anyone else?

Donalbain: [*Aside to Malcolm.*] What could we say just now, and in this place, when we know not whether danger is lurking around us, too, in the smallest and most unsuspected hiding place? We must flee. We have no time to weep.

Malcolm: [*Aside to Donalbain.*] No, our deep grief has not yet begun to make itself felt.

Banquo: Attend to Lady Macbeth.

[*Lady Macbeth is carried out.*]

We feel the chilly air. Let us return when we are fully clothed, and discuss this terrible business together, so that we may discover all that can be known of it. We are agitated by doubt and distress. For my part, I place myself in the hands of the Almighty, and fearlessly, from that standpoint, I will combat with all my power against secret plots and hidden treachery.

Macduff: I do the same.

All: We will all do so.

Macbeth: Let us arm ourselves quickly, and meet in the hall.

All: Agreed.

[Exit all but Malcolm and Donalbain.]

Malcolm: What will be our best course? We had better not accompany them. We have no means of knowing whether this show of horror and grief is real or only simulated. It is an easy thing for a deceitful person to counterfeit the appearance of sorrow. I shall make my way to England.

Donalbain: If we separate, our enemies will not be so likely to attack us singly, as it would be of no use to remove the one without the other, so I shall go to Ireland. Here, we cannot trust any. The fairest welcome may conceal the most murderous designs. True, we are surrounded by our kinsfolk, but that only places us in greater peril. It would be to the interest of some of them to remove us also.

Malcolm: Yes, it is not likely that those who have begun this fatal business will end it here, so we had better be out of the reach of their further designs. We must mount and go away, without being particular about saying farewell. This is no time for proper ceremony. We have a good excuse for our conduct, in the necessity which forces us to guard our own lives.

[Exit.]

ACT II · SCENE 4

[Outside Macbeth's castle.]
[Enter Ross and an old man.]

Old Man: My memory carries me back distinctly for seventy years and, in that period, I have witnessed many unusual and unaccountable events, and passed through terrible times. But this night of trouble and dire distress has cast all previous occurrences into the shade.

Ross: Yes, you may notice, worthy old man, how the powers above, displeased by the wicked deeds of mortal men, darkly menace the earth, on which such villainy is accomplished.

The hour tells us that day should now have arrived. Nevertheless, darkness still covers it, and chokes the struggling sunbeams. It is difficult to tell whether night has been given power to reign over this dreadful day, or whether day would rather hide itself in darkness and conceal the wicked deed from every eye. By now, the face of nature should be basking in the glad brightness of heaven.

Old Man: It is against all natural laws, as is the foul murder that has been committed. But a parallel to it occured recently, when a lordly falcon, at its utmost height of strength and speed, was chased by a far inferior bird, the owl, whose usual prey is the defenceless, timid mouse. Yet the royal bird was brought down and done to death.

Ross: Another most unaccountable thing, yet vouched for as undeniably true, is that the horses of the king, the best of all their kind, famed for their speed and beauty of form, suddenly changed their disposition, and became fierce, stubborn creatures. They broke loose from their stables and, refusing to obey any call, galloped wildly away, as if bent on bringing destruction to any who crossed their path.

Old Man: I heard a report that they attacked and devoured each other.

Ross: That is true. I myself saw it, with the most utter astonishment.

[Enter Macduff.]

Here is the noble thane of Fife. How are things going on now, my lord?

Macduff: You can see that for yourself, can you not?

Ross: I mean, has anything more come to light as to how this horrible crime was committed?

Macduff: It is certain that it must have been the king's own attendants, whom Macbeth slew.

Ross: How dreadful! What benefit did they imagine they would reap from such a deed?

Macduff: Someone had bribed them to do it. And, as the king's sons have secretly taken to flight, they are suspected of having been the instigators.

Ross: Another contradiction of natural laws! Men led astray by love of power do not perceive how wasteful they are in destroying and devouring greedily that which would have nourished their own existence and brought them nearer their desired ends, if left alone. They merely hinder their own plans in trying to accomplish them more speedily. I suppose, then, that Macbeth will now succeed to the throne.

Macduff: The nobles have already nominated him, and his coronation is to take place at Scone immediately.

Ross: What has been done with the king's dead body?

Macduff: It has been taken away for burial and sent to Iona, where the bodies of his ancestors rest in that holy place.

Ross: Do you intend to go to Scone?

Macduff: No, my friend. I shall return home to Fife.

Ross: I shall go to see the coronation.

Macduff: I hope you will find that all is right, and everything carried out in a suitable manner. Farewell. We may yet find the new regime not quite so easy to live under as the former.

Ross: Adieu, good old man.

Old Man: A heavenly blessing rest upon you, and upon all who try to benefit others by turning them from enemies into allies, and from evil ways to the love of righteousness.

[*Exit.*]

ACT III · SCENE 1

[Forres. The palace.]
[Enter Banquo.]

Banquo: Well, all is fulfilled now. All is within thy grasp, even as the fateful three predicted. First, thy titles of Glamis and Cawdor, then, finally, this of king. I cannot but suspect that this last one was obtained by treachery. And, even then, the prediction was that the sovereignty would not remain in thy family, but would pass to my descendants and that I would be the founder of a new dynasty. If I may trust their words, as I think I may, on seeing how truly they have foretold thy glory and advancement, I may encourage myself with the hope that their words to me will also be fulfilled. But silence!

[Trumpets sound. Enter Macbeth, as king:
Lady Macbeth, as queen;
Lennox, Ross, lords, ladies and attendants.]

Macbeth: Here is the friend who shall be most honored at our feast.

Lady Macbeth: Had Banquo been left out, our rejoicings would have been incomplete. Nothing could have made up for his absence, and a sense of something lacking would have pervaded all our gaiety.

Macbeth: We intend to hold a formal banquet this evening, my lord, to which we cordially invite you.

Banquo: I am at Your Majesty's service, and bound to it by the most indestructible links of loyalty and devotion.

Macbeth: Do you intend to ride abroad today?

Banquo: I do, Your Highness.

Macbeth: We would otherwise have been glad of your presence at our deliberations, for your counsel has always been marked by the greatest wisdom and by the most fortunate results, when followed. However, we shall hope for your aid tomorrow. Do you intend to go any long distance?

Banquo: The ride I am taking will require all the time from now until the hour of the feast. And, should my horse not travel well, I am afraid I shall be overtaken by darkness before I can return to the palace.

Macbeth: Do not disappoint us with your absence from the banquet.

Banquo: Your Highness, I will be there.

Macbeth: It is reported that one of the guilty sons of Duncan is now staying in England and the other in Ireland. They have not acknowledged their inhuman murder of their father, but are spreading false accounts of the occurrence to all who will listen to them. But we will leave that for consideration tomorrow, when there will also be other business to discuss on matters connected with the government, which will require our presence. Let me not hinder you now. Hurry to your ride. Farewell for the present. Are you taking your son with you?

Banquo: Yes, Your Majesty, and it is time we had set out.

Macbeth: Well, a pleasant and safe ride to you! May your steeds carry you well.

[Exit Banquo.]

Let each one do exactly as he desires, and follow his own inclinations freely, until the evening. We shall retire alone, and remain apart until the hour of the feast that we may better enjoy the conversation with others after an interval of seclusion. Until then, God keep you.

[Exit all but Macbeth and an attendant.]

Here, my good fellow. Are those men waiting?

Attendant: Your Majesty, they wait outside the gates.

Macbeth: Lead them here.

[Exit attendant.]

It is not enough to be king. I must secure myself in that position against any possible mischance. Banquo is the man whom I dread most. He has that in his noble nature which rises above me, and intimidates me. He is absolutely fearless, and yet has discretion enough to keep him from any rash act which would place him in my power. I fear no man living except Banquo. My spirit instinctively feels that he is my superior, as that famous Roman, Mark Antony, felt regarding the great Julius Caesar.

When the weird women met us, and gave me the title of king, he boldy rebuked them for not extending similar good fortune to him. Then they predicted that he would be the founder of a new royal house. All they gave to me was the bare kingship, without successors of my own to follow me, the mockery of an empty power, which soon would pass to another line, with no heir of my house following me on the throne. If this comes to pass, then I have defiled and stained my soul only to give advantage to Banquo's heirs. For his children have I raised my hand against the good and kindly monarch whom I slew. For them have I filled my bosom with rankling, soul-searing thoughts that will not be laid to rest, and lost my peace of mind forever. I have delivered my immortal soul into the power of Satan only to raise them to the throne; to raise Banquo's descendants to the position which my own should occupy. Never! Before that shall be, I will match myself against fate. Destiny itself must challenge me to mortal combat, and I will fight it to the death! Who is that outside?

[*Re-enter attendant, with two murderers.*]

Return and guard the door. I will call when I require you.

[*Exit attendant.*]

It was yesterday that we held our conversation, was it not?

First Murderer: Yes, Your Majesty.

Macbeth: Have you thought over what I told you then? It was Banquo by whom you were so oppressed and downtrodden formerly, and you attributed your misfortunes to my ill will, but I was entirely guiltless in the matter. I explained that to your satisfaction at our previous meeting, and proved to you how you had been deceived, held down and frustrated. Also, by what means it had been done, and those who used the means, until even the weakest intellect and the dullest mind could not but be convinced that you owed all your troubles to Banquo.

First Murderer: You told us all this.

Macbeth: I told you more, and that brings me to the subject of which I wish to speak in this, our second, conference. Are you meek and forgiving enough to pass over these injuries? Are you so well governed by the precepts of the gospel as to offer your petitions to heaven on behalf of this benefactor of yours, and of his children, when it is owing to his oppression that you are brought so low, and your little ones are in want and poverty?

First Murderer: Your Highness, we have the feelings of men.

Macbeth: Yes, but men are of many different kinds. No doubt you rank among the general class—"man". In the same way, we give the generic name of "dogs" to all the various

32

kinds of hounds, swift or strong, to dogs of mixed breed, Spanish dogs, worthless and degenerate dogs, rough-haired dogs, shaggy water hounds and dogs which have the nature of wolves. But, in the carefully compiled catalogue, in which all their qualities and prices are set forth, each one worthy of it has a distinctive title according to his special attributes. One is speedy and alert, another not so brisk, another intelligent and clever, another a trustworthy watchdog, another skilful in tracking game, and so on. Now, to which list do you belong? If you are not among the dregs of humanity, but are worthy of a place in the catalogue of individual worth, let me know. I will unfold to your minds a plan of action which, if you carry it out, will remove from your path the one who has done you so much injury, and bind me to you in the strongest gratitude and regard. My own life and well-being will never be safe from risk of danger and attack so long as he lives. But, were he dead, I would be absolutely secure.

Second Murderer: Your Majesty, I have had so hard a life and have met with so many misfortunes that I am filled with rage against fate, and am ready to do anything to gratify my desire for revenge.

First Murderer: I, too, am worn out by struggling against misfortune. I am so disheartened that I care not what risks I run. I will take any hazard that offers the opportunity of either bettering my condition or ending my life once and for all.

Macbeth: You are each aware that Banquo was a foe to you.

Both Murderers: We know it, sir.

Macbeth: He is also an enemy of mine, and is so widely alienated from me, and possessed of so deadly a hatred against me, that my very existence is threatened every moment that he lives. My position gives me power to remove him from my path openly, and boldly state that it was my sovereign will. But I prefer not to do so, on account of many of my own followers, who are also friends of Banquo and whom I cannot afford to lose. For this reason, I must even mourn and lament his death, although it takes place by my own orders. Therefore, it was necessary that I should invite your kind co-operation, in order that the plan might be carried out secretly, for several important considerations.

Second Murderer: Your Majesty, your instructions shall be strictly obeyed.

First Murderer: Even should it be our fate . . .

Macbeth: Your courage is plainly apparent. In a very short time I will tell you where to take up your position, and let you know the best place to watch for the moment of his arrival. The deed must be accomplished this very evening, and at some considerable distance from my residence. It must always be understood that I must be perfectly clear from any suspicion of involvement in the murder. And, in order that there may be no imperfections in your work, but that the whole thing may be completed satisfactorily, Banquo's son, who accompanies him, must share the same dreadful doom. The removal of Fleance is as essential to my plans as is that of Banquo. Think it over by yourselves, and let me know your decision. I will return to you presently.

Both Murderers: Our decision is made, Your Highness.

Macbeth: I shall require you soon, then. Wait inside awhile.

[Exit murderers.]

Banquo, thy fate is decided! If thou art to enter the home of the blessed, thou wilt enter within a few short hours.

[Exit.]

ACT III · SCENE 2

[The palace.]
[Enter Lady Macbeth and a servant.]

Lady Macbeth: Do you know whether Banquo has departed?

Servant: Yes, Your Majesty. But he comes back again this evening.

Lady Macbeth: Let His Majesty know that I would like to have some conversation with him, at his convenience.

Servant: I shall do so, madam.

[Exit.]

Lady Macbeth: It is all to no avail. We gain nothing whatever by the attainment of our dearest wishes when we are not able to enjoy them with a mind at peace. It would even be better to have been brought to destruction ourselves, than to live in such an atmosphere of suspense and dread on account of having destroyed others.

Why is this, my husband? Why do you remain in solitude, with only wretched thoughts and dismal memories for company? You should have dismissed them all on the death of Duncan. It is no use brooding over things that cannot be mended. The deed, once committed, is irrevocable.

Macbeth: That deed only partly ensured our safety. It did not make us secure. The wounds we gave to danger will heal, and it will rise against us as menacingly as ever, while our feeble and useless attempts to parry its thrusts will leave us no safer than before. But I will no longer allow myself to be a prey to these fears and terrors. Let this firmly established universe fall to pieces, and heaven and earth come to ruin together, before we will live our daily lives in dread, and fear to sleep for fear of terrifying visions of the brain. To lie at rest with the quiet dead, to whom we gave a calm and peaceful sleep, vainly imagining that we would secure peace for ourselves, would be infinitely preferable to living thus, in a continual agony of excitement and fear. The king lies at rest in his tomb, in deep and calm repose, after the restless turmoil of his mortal life. Nothing now can disturb his sleep. Treachery cannot injure him further, neither weapon nor deadly drug can reach him. Civil wars and foreign invaders are all powerless to break his peaceful rest.

Lady Macbeth: My dear husband, come with me to our friends. Smooth the expression of your features, and be happy, friendly and genial in their company.

Macbeth: I will, dearest wife, and you do likewise. Do not forget to single out Banquo for special distinction, both by words and looks. Only because our position is not yet firmly established do we stoop our dignity to flatter him thus. Our faces must, like masks, show a false friendliness, while concealing the real feelings of our hearts.

Lady Macbeth: You really must cease to think of this subject.

Macbeth: Beloved, my heart is tortured and stung by thoughts of fear. Thou art aware that Banquo yet lives, and his son.

Lady Macbeth: True, but they are not immortal.

Macbeth: Neither are they invulnerable. There is some consolation in that. Be merry, dear wife. This night, before the dusk-loving bat comes forth to fly in the dim woods and before the beetle, borne on scaly wings, drones his sleepy signal at the call of the dark night goddess, an act of terrible infamy will be perpetrated, a deed that shall ring in men's ears.

Lady Macbeth: Oh! What do you intend?

Macbeth: It is better that you should know nothing about it beforehand, sweet wife. You will applaud later, when you hear what has been done. Come, soft darkness, that closes the eye of wearied day. Cover up and blind the vision of the compassionate hours of light, so that they do not look upon the deed that is to be done. An unseen murderous stroke shall rend and destroy the lease of that life which keeps me subject to continual fears. Night closes in, the crow seeks her nest in the trees and all the innocent creatures that belong to the hours of light are preparing themselves for sleep, while the evil things of darkness awaken and go forth to their work of death. Thou art amazed at what I say, but remain patient for a time. When a course of evil is once embarked on, we can only avoid the consequences of our first misdeeds by plunging still deeper into crime. Come, I pray you.

[*Exit.*]

ACT III · SCENE 3

[*A park near the palace.*]
[*Enter three murderers.*]

First Murderer: Who sent you here?

Third Murderer: The king.

Second Murderer: Then it will be all right. We need not be afraid to trust him. He knows exactly what we have been ordered to do, in every particular. He could not know this except from Macbeth himself.

First Murderer: Very well, remain in our company, then. There are still a few faint gleams of daylight in the western sky. Those who are journeying and are likely to be overtaken by darkness now quicken their horses' pace to gain welcome hospitality in time. Here comes the one for whom we are watching.

Third Murderer: Listen! I hear the beat of horses' hoofs.

Banquo: [*Within.*] Let us have one of your torches.

Second Murderer: It can be no other than Banquo because all the other invited guests have already arrived.

First Murderer: The horses are going in another direction.

Third Murderer: Yes, they have a circuit of nearly a mile to travel. Banquo generally walks from here to the entrance of the palace. So, indeed, do most people.

Second Murderer: Here they come! I see their torches.

[Enter Banquo, and Fleance with a torch.]

Third Murderer: Yes, it is Banquo.

First Murderer: Be ready.

Banquo: We shall have rain shortly.

First Murderer: Let it come down!

[They set upon Banquo.]

Banquo: O treason! Villainy! Escape, my son! Flee for thy life! Thou may yet avenge thy father! O villain!

[Dies. Fleance escapes.]

Third Murderer: Who put out the torch?

First Murderer: Should I not have done so?

Third Murderer: We have only killed one. The younger one has escaped.

Second Murderer: We have left the most important part of our work undone.

First Murderer: Well, let us go and report what we have accomplished.

[Exit.]

ACT III · SCENE 4

[A hall in the palace.]

[A banquet prepared. Enter Macbeth, Lady Macbeth, Ross, Lennox, lords and attendants.]

Macbeth: Gentlemen, be seated. You all know your order of precedence, and now I bid you a cordial welcome, one and all.

Lords: Our thanks, Your Highness.

Macbeth: We will join you at the board and sit among you. Her Majesty remains in her chair of state for the present but, in good time, she also will descend and greet you.

Lady Macbeth: Give my cordial welcome to all our guests now, my lord. From my heart, I greet them.

[First murderer appears at the door.]

Macbeth: They return your good wishes most heartily. See, I will here take my seat among you, an equal number on each hand. Be merry, friends, and presently we shall drink to each other throughout the company. [*Approaching the door.*] Your face is stained with blood!

Murderer: It belongs to Banquo, then.

Macbeth: Well, the blood is better on thee than still in his body. Is he dead?

Murderer: Your Highness, I killed him myself, by cutting his throat.

Macbeth: Thou art the prince of all murderers. Yet the one who did the same to Fleance is equally good. If thou did both, thou art above all comparison the best. Thou art unequalled.

Murderer: Banquo's son succeeded in getting away, Your Majesty.

Macbeth: [*Aside.*] Then I am seized with uneasy fear once more. But for that I would have been as firmly established as the solid rock, as free in spirit as the surrounding air. Now, I cannot feel that I am free to move in safety. I am still trapped and surrounded by impertinent and troublesome fears and apprehensions.

You are sure that Banquo is effectively disposed of?

Murderer: Yes, Your Majesty. He lies in a hollow by the roadside, with a score of gaping wounds upon him, even the smallest of which would have been sufficient to cause his death.

Macbeth: I am grateful for so much, at least. [*Aside.*] The old viper is safely accounted for. The young one that has escaped can do no harm just yet, although, being the son of his father, he will certainly sting in the future. Depart for the present. We will speak together tomorrow.

[*Exit murderer.*]

Lady Macbeth: My king, you do not speak words of welcome to your guests. It is necessary to repeat your kindly assurances more frequently, or the banquet will be no better than a meal purchased at an inn. It is the observance of the rules of cordial interplay between host and guests that gives enjoyment to a feast when partaken of in another person's house. If that be wanting, the banquet becomes a mere cold and formal reception, and as far as the actual eating is concerned, one would enjoy one's meals better at home.

Macbeth: Dearest love, I thank you for your kindly reminder. We hope that all will partake of our feast with the zest of a healthy hunger, and that no after-effects will detract from your enjoyment of it, but that it may add to your strength of manhood.

Lennox: Will Your Majesty be pleased to join us now?

[*The ghost of Banquo enters, and sits in Macbeth's place.*]

Macbeth: If only our honored Banquo were now here, the noblest company in all Scotland would be assembled within these walls. I am inclined to blame him for his absence rather than sympathize with him for any accident that was likely to detain him.

Ross: Indeed, my liege, he has shown himself guilty of breaking his word. May it please Your Majesty to honor us with your gracious presence at the table?

Macbeth: There is no room.

Lennox: Yes, my liege. Here is a vacant seat kept for you.

Macbeth: Which seat?

Lennox: This one, gracious lord. Why is Your Majesty so agitated?

Macbeth: Who has caused this to be done?

Lords: Caused what, dear lord?

Macbeth: There is no proof that I am to blame. Do not shake your bleeding head at me!

Ross: My lords, let us go. His Majesty is ill.

Lady Macbeth: I pray you, my good lords, remain. The king is subject to these attacks, and has been, since he was young. It will soon pass. He will recover in a few moments; do not rise. Proceed with the banquet. If he sees you observing him, it will only make him worse, and probably cause his anger to fall upon you.

Do you call yourself a man?

Macbeth: Yes, and not a coward, either. But I confess I fear a sight like this, which might terrify Satan himself.

Lady Macbeth: This is sheer nonsense! It is pure imagination, conjured up by your fears, as when you told me you saw the image of a dagger in the air, which directed you to the sleeping king. This is more of the same sort—a brain picture of your terrors. These commotions of mind and sudden movements of terror are mere pretences, compared with the manifestations of a real dread. They are worthy of women sitting round the hearth hearing a winter's tale of ghosts, given on the authority of an old grandmother! It is a disgrace to you! Can you not keep your facial expression better than that? After all, there is nothing but a seat to gaze at.

Macbeth: But look! See, I beg you! There! What can you say to that? Well, I care not. You can surely speak, if you can move. If our dead are to be given back again to earth from their vaults and resting places in this manner, we must henceforth give them to be devoured by the birds of prey, and make sure that they cannot return.

[Ghost vanishes.]

Lady Macbeth: Is your manhood entirely driven out of you by this utter foolishness?

Macbeth: I really saw him, as surely as I am in this place.

Lady Macbeth: You ought to be ashamed to say so.

Macbeth: People have been murdered before this, in former days, before kindlier and juster laws had been passed, for the ensuring of the better safety of the commonwealth. And, even since those days, men have been done to death in dreadful manner. But, when they were killed once, all was over; the transaction was completed. Now, it seems that killing is not enough. They reappear, with all their wounds upon them and throw us from our places. A murder is not such an unheard-of occurrence. It is the reappearance that is to be wondered at.

Lady Macbeth: My dear husband, your guests wait for you. They miss your attentions, as their host.

Macbeth: I had forgotten them.

Dear friends, do not be surprised, and wonder at what has taken place. I am subject to this weakness. Those who are acquainted with me have ceased to be surprised at it. I wish affection and well-being to everyone. Bring wine, and fill the measure to the brim. I will take my seat when we have drunk this pledge: happiness and all good wishes to each one here, not forgetting our beloved Banquo, whose absence we feel deeply, and whose presence we greatly desire. We drink to you all!

Lords: Our loyal service to you. We drink to you!

[Re-enter ghost.]

Macbeth: Begone! Let me not see thee! Thou should lie beneath the earth. Thy bones are empty of their life's substance, there is no warmth in thy blood, no sight or intelligence in those eyes, which stare so fixedly at me!

Lady Macbeth: Kind nobles, pray do not think that is an unusual occurrence. It frequently happens. My only regret is that it should dampen your enjoyment of the present occasion.

Macbeth: I fear no adversary that may be fought by human means. Come in the form of the fiercest wild beast; the shaggy bear of the Russian woods; the rhinoceros, with his thick skin and horned head; or the ravenous tiger of Hyrcania, and I will meet thee readily. Come in any form but this spectral image, and thou shalt never make me shiver. Or come back to life and earth once more, and challenge me to meet thee blade to blade in the most desolate spot, none but ourselves being near. And, if I am frightened before thee then, call me no warrior, but the weakest child! Away, dreadful ghost! Shadowy apparition, begone!

[*Ghost vanishes.*]

There! I am once more master of myself, now that it has departed. Do not rise, friends, I beg.

Lady Macbeth: You have destroyed all the pleasure of the evening. Our assembly is now effectively broken up in wondering commotion.

Macbeth: When things like this take place so unexpectedly and overshadow us like a thundercloud in summer, can you expect us not to be amazed? I am constrained to wonder at the state of my own feelings when I see you able to look on a spectacle like that without turning pale, when terror has chased the blood from my cheeks.

Ross: What spectacle have you seen, Your Highness?

Lady Macbeth: Do not address him, please, it will only anger him. I fear he is becoming worse. I pray you, gentlemen, go now. Do not wait for the strict order of court ceremonial, but leave us quickly.

Lennox: Farewell, lady. May His Majesty soon recover.

Lady Macbeth: Our loving farewells to you all.

[*Exit all but Macbeth and Lady Macbeth*]

Macbeth: O, it will be revenged upon us; it will recoil upon our heads; it cannot be concealed! When other evidence has been lacking, the lifeless things of nature have been endowed with power to point out the guilty. By the reading of omens and signs, and the careful tracing of effect to cause, by divination by means of crows, ravens and magpies, the most hidden crime has been discovered, and the profoundest secret brought to life.

How far has the night advanced?

Lady Macbeth: So far that it is almost morning.

Macbeth: What do you think of the thane of Fife refusing to attend the court at our royal summons?

Lady Macbeth: Have you commanded him, my lord?

Macbeth: Not yet openly, but I intend to do so. I hear this news in an indirect way. I have secret spies in my pay in every castle. Early tomorrow I shall pay a visit to the fateful three. I shall compel them to tell me more, for I am determined to know my fate, by foul means, if I cannot learn it otherwise. I will sweep from my path every obstruction that stands in the way of my own interests. I have advanced so far in crime that to retrace my steps now would be as difficult as to continue in the same career of guilt. I have other plans in my mind, too, which will need to be carried out. But they must be performed before they can be examined, for they are of such a nature that they will not bear close scrutiny.

Lady Macbeth: You are greatly in need of slumber, the chief preservative of all living beings.

Macbeth: Let us go to rest. These deceiving feelings and emotions of my mind are due to the fact that I am not yet hardened in sin. They are the terrors of the beginner in crime.

[*Exit.*]

ACT III · SCENE 5

[*A heath.*]
[*Thunder. Enter the three witches, meeting Hecate.*]

First Witch: What is wrong, Hecate? You seem to be angry.

Hecate: You have given me good cause, you presumptuous old hags! What right had you to carry out all that business of deceiving Macbeth with confusing ideas and suggestions of murder, while I, your instructress, the one from whom you learn your spells, and who invents all those secret forms of mischief which you carry out, knew nothing of it, and was never given an opportunity to display my powers of enchantment? More annoying, still, you chose to aid with your spells one who is utterly selfish and passionate. He only listens to you as far as it will serve his own interests. You must do your best now to repair your error. Begone, but be in the cave at the mouth of the lower regions early tomorrow. Have your spells and your cauldrons ready, and all that is necessary to deceive him further.

I go to fly through the air. I will occupy the hours of darkness in preparing for his dreadful fate. There is work of great importance to be done, and quickly. There is a wondrous drop of fluid ready to fall from the moon. I will catch it before it reaches the earth. Its mystical qualities are such that it will help me, by my arts, to present to Macbeth such false and deceptive appearances that he will be still further led astray, and rush headlong to ruin. In the fancied security that he will gather from our words, he will defy destiny, and challenge death to do its worst, thinking that the knowledge that he possesses lifts him above the necessity of being guided by holy words of counsel and virtue. An imagined immunity from attack is a most potent factor in bringing about the ruin of men and nations, as you are well aware.

[*Music and a song within: "Come away, come away," etc.*]

Listen! My familiar spirit summons me away. It is waiting for me, wrapped in the mist.

[*Exit.*]

First Witch: Let us begin our task quickly. It will not be long before she returns.

[*Exit.*]

ACT III · SCENE 6

[*Forres. The palace.*]
[*Enter Lennox with another lord.*]

Lennox: What I have already told you is sufficient to set your mind upon the track, and I have no doubt you will be able to discover further meanings for yourself. All I will say is that very significant occurrences have taken place. Macbeth lamented greatly over Duncan, but Duncan was safely dead by that time. And the brave and valorous general, Banquo, stayed out too long. People should not run risks like walking abroad at all hours of the night. His son ran away, so you may take it that his son was the murderer, if you choose. Everyone will agree that it was a most dreadful crime for Duncan's two sons to murder their loving parent—an accursed deed! Macbeth was beside himself with grief and, in his attack of sacred sorrow, he instantly stabbed the two culprits who had allowed themselves to be held in bondage by wine and slumber. Do you not think that was a good deed, and rightly done? Yes, and it was also a very clever one. Who would not have been indignant when the men protested their innocence? Oh yes! He has managed everything splendidly. If it please God, he shall never have Malcolm and Donalbain in his power. But, if he had, he would soon show them, and Banquo's son also, what punishment is given out to children who slay their fathers.

But we must say nothing, for the thane of Fife has found out what is the result of speaking his mind freely. Both, for that and because he absented himself from the banquet, he is now under Macbeth's deepest displeasure. Do you happen to know, my lord, where he is at present?

Lord: Malcolm, who is kept out of his birthright by the usurper, Macbeth, is now at the court of England. There, the saintly king has welcomed him kindly, and, although exiled and fallen on evil days, he is treated with all the deference and respect due to his high rank.

Macduff has gone there too, in order to ask good King Edward to grant him the help of the valiant Earl of Northumbria, and to ask him to raise a tax in his earldom, so that by their aid, and with the blessing of God upon their efforts, we may once more sleep securely, enjoy a sufficiency of food in our own houses, banish the fear of assassination from our assemblies, pay our loyal service to a king worthy of it and be able to accept his rewards as free and faithful subjects. We can do none of these things under the present regime. Macbeth has heard this news. He is furiously angry and is making preparations to take the field in combat.

Lennox: Did he invite Macduff's presence?

Lord: Yes, and Macduff answered flatly, "Sir, I will not!" The man who brought the king's message turned away frowning, with an ''Ahem!'' which seemed to suggest that it would be the worse for the noble thane when that response was carried to the king.

Lennox: That would certainly warn him to get as far away from Macbeth as possible. May some good spirit put it into the heart of the king of England to set about this business even before Macduff's arrival, so that our unhappy land may have less time to wait for deliverance from this intolerable tyranny!

Lord: My earnest petitions shall go along with him.

[*Exit.*]

ACT IV · SCENE 1
[A cavern. In the middle, a boiling cauldron.]
[Thunder. Enter the three witches.]

First Witch: The streaked and spotted cat has cried three times.

Second Witch: And four times has the hedgehog sounded its plaintive cry.

Third Witch: The hour has come, Harpy calls.

First Witch: Circle around the simmering pot. Cast in the poisoned entrails. Cast first into the magic cauldron the toad that has sweated its own poisonous perspiration for many days under the icy rocks.

All: Increase twofold, all labor and pain, while the flames leap around the boiling vessel.

Second Witch: Take now a slice from the flesh of a snake caught in the foul marshes; the eye of a newt and the toe severed from a frog; hair from the night-flying bat, and a dog's tongue; the forked tongue of a viper, and a blindworm's sting; the leg of a lizard, and wing of an owl. Boil them all together in the cauldron, an infernal mixture for our wicked spells.

All: Swell and grow, evil work and dire misfortune, while the flames dance around the simmering cauldron.

Third Witch: Take now a thick scale from the fierce dragon; the tooth of a ravening wolf; the dried body of a sorceress; the mouth and stomach of the devouring shark, filled with prey; the root of the deadly hemlock plant, obtained in the deepest night; the liver of an unbeliever; the bile from a goat; some splinters torn from the poisonous yew tree, when the moon was hidden from the earth; the nose and lips of marauding Asiatics; the finger of an infant born of a prostitute in a ditch, and strangled at birth; mingle all together, and make the mixture thick and slimy. Now add to the rest the entrails of a tiger.

All: Yet more and more, multiply all disaster and dread, while the devouring flames surround the seething cauldron.

Second Witch: Take the blood of an ape and cool the mixture. Now, our awful spell is powerful and complete.

[Enter Hecate.]

Hecate: You have done bravely. I praise you now for your work. Each shall receive a share of the reward. Now, surround the boiling cauldron like elfish spirits, and, with your song, cast a yet stronger spell over all within it.

[*Music and a song: "Black spirits," etc. Hecate retires.*]

Second Witch: I feel, by the sensation of something sharp piercing my thumbs, that some evil thing is approaching. Barriers, give way to those who seek entrance.

Macbeth: What are you doing, you dark and mysterious beings?

All: No words may tell our deed.

Macbeth: By the supernatural knowledge that you say you possess, in whatever manner you obtained it, I order you to reply to my questions. I care not, though you loose the winds from their bonds, and they rage until they destroy the places of our holy worship, until the foaming waves bring every vessel to destruction, until the growing grain be laid flat in the fields, and the mighty trees are uprooted, until the fortress walls are blown down about the ears of the guards, until the strong residences of kings and huge, secure structures bow their heads and are overthrown. I care not, though all the lavish abundance of every green and growing thing throughout the land be blasted and withered, until ruin itself is complete. I dare all this, so that you may answer my demands.

First Witch: Let us hear.

Second Witch: Make your request.

Third Witch: You shall have a reply.

First Witch: Would thou prefer to hear thy answer from us, or from the lips of the powerful spirits who govern us?

Macbeth: Bring them forth. Show them to me.

First Witch: Add to the cauldron the blood of a sow that has devoured her litter of nine, and throw in, to quicken the fire, the perspiration of a murderer who was hanged.

All: Great and small, come forth. Skilfully reveal thyself and what thou can perform.

[*Thunder. First apparition—an armed head.*]

Macbeth: Mysterious spirit, let me know . . .

First Witch: He is well aware of what thou would ask. Speak not, but listen only.

First Apparition: Beware, Macbeth. Beware, great king. The thane of Fife is thine enemy. Now bid me depart.

[*Descends.*]

Macbeth: Thou hast my gratitude for thy warning, thou

unknown being. Thou hast touched on a fear already felt by me. Tell me now . . .

First Witch: He will not obey thee. Now comes a more powerful spirit.

[*Thunder. Second apparition—a bloody child.*]

Second Apparition: Macbeth! King! Monarch!

Macbeth: I would listen with all my powers, even if I had more organs of hearing than the normal number.

Second Apparition: Be fierce, be firm, be valiant. Fear no mortal enemy, and look with contempt on all human plans against thee. No man born of woman shall be able to injure Macbeth.

[*Descends.*]

Macbeth: Then I will spare the proud thane, since I need not now dread him. But, no. I will make my safety absolutely and undeniably certain, and take a pledge from destiny. I will destroy him, so that I may be able to laugh at my terrors and rest in peace at last.

[*Thunder. Third apparition—a child crowned, with a tree in his hand.*]

Who is this child, its infant brow encircled by a kingly crown?

All: Keep silent and hear its words!

Third Apparition: Be courageous, proud and arrogant. Regard none who rage and fume, or plot against thee. Nothing can conquer Macbeth until the green forest of Birnam leaves its place, and marches against him to the hill of Dunsinane.

[*Descends.*]

Macbeth: Then I shall remain invincible! For what power is there that can enlist the woods in his army, or cause the firmly fixed trees to loosen themselves from their station? Fair and encouraging prophecies! Now no revolt or foul conspiracy can disturb my reign. I shall live out my appointed time in the exalted station to which I have climbed. I shall reign in security until I breathe my last breath and take my leave of life according to the usual course of nature. But, now, I ardently desire one further piece of information. If your power extends so far, tell me if the sovereignty of this land will really pass on to Banquo's heirs?

All: Do not seek to penetrate farther into the future.

Macbeth: But I insist. Curses on you if you refuse to satisfy me in this request. Tell me at once. What terrible sounds are these, [*Low musical sounds.*] and why is the cauldron disappearing?

First Witch: Reveal to him!

Second Witch: Display the sight!

Third Witch: Disclose the future!

All: Manifest thyself to his sight, and cause him sorrow and anger. Appear and disappear in spectral fashion.

[*A show of eight kings, the last with a glass in his hand. Banquo's ghost following.*]

Macbeth: Away! Thou bear too strong a resemblance to Banquo. My eyes are blasted by the sight of thy regal adornments. Thou, too, thou second form. Thy locks are like the former, and are enclosed by the same royal circlet, and a similar form follows after. Wretched sorceresses! Is this what I asked to see? Yet another! My eyes will spring from their sockets at this appalling sight. Still more! Is the line endless? Will it continue until the thunder of the judgment day? And yet a sixth, and another following! I will look no longer. Now follows an eighth and, in his hand, a mirror in which I behold many others yet to come. Some of them bear two spheres, and others a threefold mace, the sign of extended dominion, in their hands. Hateful spectacle! But now I perceive that you have shown me truly, for Banquo, with bloodclotted hair, points to them, smiling, indicating that they are his posterity. [*Apparitions vanish.*] Will all this come to pass?

First Witch: Yea, king. It will come to pass. But do not let it depress and bewilder you so. Come, my companions, let us put forth our best efforts and revive his drooping spirits. By a spell, I will cause music to be heard in the air, while you go through the figures of an ancient dance, so that we may render to this mighty monarch the ceremonious service due to his rank.

[*Music. The witches dance, and then vanish, with Hecate.*]

Macbeth: Have they vanished? A curse remain forever on this malignant and evil day! Enter, you who wait outside.

[*Enter Lennox.*]

Lennox: What does Your Highness command?

Macbeth: Did you see the witches?

Lennox: I did not, Your Majesty.

Macbeth: Did they not pass you?

Lennox: I am certain they did not, my liege.

Macbeth: May the air be polluted by their presence wherever they go, and accursed be all those who put faith in their false sayings! Who rode past? I heard the sound of horsemen.

Lennox: It was some messengers, sire, who came to tell you that the thane of Fife has taken refuge in England.

Macbeth: Gone to England?

Lennox: Yes, Your Majesty.

Macbeth: [*Aside.*] Thou art quicker than me, time, and hast prevented me from carrying out my evil plan. After this, I will execute my plans the instant that I conceive them. Unless the intention is put into action at once, the fleeting time slips past and is never overtaken. I will do what remains even yet. I will carry out the rest of my purpose immediately. I will order the thane's castle in Fife to be seized, confiscate his lands and deliver over to death his children, with Lady Macduff, and any other unhappy beings who are related to him. I shall not let this end in mere talk, but give the necessary orders before the fire of my anger dies out. But never again will I seek to see into the future!

Where have the messengers gone? Take me to them.

[*Exit.*]

ACT IV · SCENE 2

[*Fife. Macduff's castle.*]
[*Enter Lady Macduff, her son and Ross.*]

Lady Macduff: Has my husband done anything wrong? Why has he had to flee from his country?

Ross: Dear lady, be patient.

Lady Macduff: Macduff was not patient. It was an insane act to flee like that. His fear will lead him to be called a traitor, although he has given no cause by his deeds.

Ross: You cannot tell whether this step was dictated by prudence and good sense, or by a doubt of his safety.

Lady Macduff: Good sense! Was it sensible, do you think, to leave his spouse, his children, his castle and all the dues of his rank, and flee to a place where he has none of these things? He cannot care for us. He is without the ordinary feelings of affection. The birds of the air might teach him a lesson in this. Even the tiny wren will fight gallantly for her offspring against the attack of birds of prey. There has been no affection in the case. He has been ruled entirely by fear, and there is as little good sense as affection, seeing that his action in leaving his home is so causeless and unreasonable.

Ross: Beloved cousin, do not lose control over your feelings, I beg you. As for Macduff, he does not deserve your blame. He is honorable and prudent, and he possesses sound judgment. Morever, he is better acquainted with the critical situation of the hour than you can be. I cannot tell you my meaning more openly. To what a condition are we now reduced, when we are looked upon as traitors, yet are ignorant of being so ourselves, when we believe every report that flies, being inclined to do so by our continual fears. Yet our very apprehensions are so vague that we can scarcely define them, but are tossed about by sudden and stormy events, whichever way we move. I will say farewell now, but it shall not be many days before I return. Take comfort. Your troubles may end soon, and you will be left in peace, or your fortunes may mend, and reach the same height of prosperity as formerly. All good wishes be upon you, my sweet little kinsman!

Lady Macduff: He is practically an orphan, although he has a father.

Ross: If I remain longer, I would disgrace myself and distress you by foolish and unmanly tears, so I will bid you farewell.

[Exit.]

Lady Macduff: Well, little fellow, you have lost your father. What will become of you now? What will you do for food?

Son: The same as the birds, mother.

Lady Macduff: Will you eat worms and insects?

Son: I mean, I will live on whatever I can get. That is what they do.

Lady Macduff: Poor little bird! Would thou not be afraid of being caught by poison, or in a net, or snare or trap?

Son: Indeed, no. Why should I fear them? If I were a *poor* little bird, I would not be worth catching, so no one would trouble to set traps for me. But regardless of what you say, I do not believe I have lost my father.

Lady Macduff: Yes, indeed you have. Now what will become of you without one?

Son: And what will become of you without a husband?

Lady Macduff: There is no lack of husbands. I can purchase a score of them in any public place of business.

Son: Then, if you bought them there, it would only be to dispose of them again.

Lady Macduff: Thou use all thy understanding in thy answers. And, indeed, it is understanding enough for one of thy years.

Son: Mother, is it true that my father was a traitor?

Lady Macduff: Yes, he was indeed.

Son: What does it mean, to be a traitor?

Lady Macduff: It means, to be deceitful and false.

Son: Is everyone who is deceitful and false a traitor?

Lady Macduff: Yes, every one, and they have to be put to death.

Son: Must all deceitful people be put to death?

Lady Macduff: Yes, all.

Son: Who has to do it?

Lady Macduff: The good, true people, of course.

Son: Then the deceitful, false people are very silly, for there are enough of them to overcome all the good ones, and put them to death instead.

Lady Macduff: Unhappy little man, heaven help thee! But now what will become of thee for lack of a father?

Son: If I really had no father, you would be mourning for him. And, if you were not, I would know that I would soon have another father.

Lady Macduff: Poor little chatterer, what things you say!

[Enter a messenger.]

Messenger: Heaven's blessing on you, noble lady! You do not know me, though I am quite well-acquainted with your name and rank. I fear you are in great and immediate peril. If you will take the advice of a humble well-wisher, you will leave this place at once, and flee with your children to some safe refuge. It is cruel of me to terrify you in this manner, but it would be greater cruelty if I did not warn you of your danger, and savage cruelty is too near you as it is. God keep you in safety! I must flee.

Lady Macduff: Alas! Where can I find refuge if I leave my own house? I have done ill to no one. But I am reminded that I am still a dweller in this world below, where it is frequently called a praiseworthy act to do injury to others, while to do right is often the height of foolishness from a worldly point of view. It is ridiculous, therefore, to put forward the feminine plea that I have never injured anyone.

[Enter murderers.]

What strange and dreadful looks are these?

First Murderer: Where is the thane of Fife?

Lady Macduff: I sincerely hope that he is not in any such degraded and unholy place as thou art likely to meet him in.

First Murderer: He is false to his king.

Son: That is not true, thou shock-headed knave.

First Murderer: What, you young son of villainy! *[Stabbing him.]* Offspring of a traitor!

Son: Oh, mother! Flee, escape. I am murdered! *[Dies.]*

[Exit Lady Macduff, crying "Murder!"
Exit murderers, following her.]

ACT IV · SCENE 3

[England. In front of the king's palace.]
[Enter Malcolm and Macduff.]

Malcolm: Come, we will go together to some lonely spot and, there, give our heavy hearts the relief of tears.

Macduff: It will be much more to the purpose if we draw the deadly weapon, and stand over our poor country like valiant soldiers defending the body of a fallen friend. With every day comes some fresh tale of widows left desolate, children losing their parents, calamities and distresses happening all around, until their cry of grief rises to heaven, and it seems to answer with words of sorrow.

Malcolm: Whatever reports I am able to put faith in, I will believe. I sincerely grieve for what I know has taken place. And, given a favorable time and opportunity, I shall do my utmost to remedy those griefs. It may be that what you tell me is correct. Yet this tyrant, whose very name burns our lips as we utter it, was once looked upon as an honorable man. You yourself had, at one time, a considerable affection for him, and he has not yet injured you. You may yet be able to do him a service and gain his gratitude by delivering me to his wrath, though it may be that Macbeth despises me because of my youth, and looks upon me as too insignificant to be worth the trouble of destroying.

Macduff: There is no treachery in my nature.

Malcolm: No, but there is in Macbeth's. And even a noble and honorable disposition may fall away from its integrity, under the pressure of a royal command. But forgive me, I beg you. Of course, your own nature cannot be affected by what I may think, but will remain unchanged. The bright beings above still shine in undimmed splendor, though the most splendid has forfeited his own estate. Even if all the evil things in the world were to put on the appearance of virtue, yet that could not alter the quality of virtue, which would still be the same as before.

Macduff: I see that my wishes are not to be realized!

Malcolm: It may be that the same considerations that cause me to doubt you have led to your disappointment in me. Why did you flee in such haste, and leave your wife and children, those dear and powerful ties that bound you to your home and country? Do not be offended with me, I beg. I only seek to know whether my suspicions are well-founded, not in order to prove that you are treacherous, but to ensure my own safety. You may be most trustworthy and honorable, no matter what my opinion is.

Macduff: My unhappy land, still must thy lifeblood be drained away by suffering and wrong! Now make thyself secure in thy seat, thou powerful despotism that holds it in thy grasp, for virtue and justice cannot hope to oppose thee. Still, bear thy injuries for there is no hope of overthrowing the tyrant's line; it is settled firmly. Adieu, sir. Not for all the wealth of the country held by the usurper, and all the untold riches of the glorious East added to it, would I be the blackhearted knave thou dost consider me.

Malcolm: Do not be displeased with me. It is not altogether because I suspect you that I have said this. I really do believe that Scotland is suffering under an intolerable tyranny. It lies groaning under an accumulation of wrongs, and I believe that were I to return and claim the throne, many would gladly fight on my side, as well as the troops that the generous Edward has offered me. Yet, when I have overthrown Macbeth and have him at my feet, or carry his head from the battlefield on the point of my sword, unhappy Scotland would be no better off than before, but rather worse. He who would reign in the usurper's place would inflict greater injuries upon it by his wickedness, and cause it to suffer in a greater variety of ways than ever before.

Macduff: And who will that be?

Malcolm: I am speaking of myself. I know my own nature, and I tell you that when my wickednesses are revealed, sinful Macbeth will appear good and pure in comparison, and the miserable country will remember him as having been gentle and harmless, when it experiences my boundless sins.

Macduff: That is impossible. Not even among the hordes of hell can there be an accursed spirit whose crimes can outweigh those of Macbeth.

Malcolm: I agree that he is cruel, voluptuous, covetous, untruthful, treacherous, malignant and of a passionate temper—in fact, infected with every evil one can recount. But my lustful passion is without bounds. Not all the women in Scotland could satisfy my appetite, or satisfy my desires, and I would sweep every restraining obstacle out of my way. Scotland would suffer less under its present tyrant than under one of such a character.

Macduff: Such unrestrained passion is a tyranny in itself, and has led to many a revolt and to the downfall of many rulers. Still, if it be so, you may contrive to satisfy even that desire in your own land and, at the same time, deceive all your countrymen by putting on an appearance of coldness. Your appetite cannot be so boundless and fierce that you cannot find the means to gratify it to the full.

Malcolm: And, also, in my wicked disposition there is such an unsatisfiable greed, that if I were monarch and had it in my power, I would condemn the lords and thanes to death on the slightest pretext, for the sake of their possessions. I would desire the treasures of one and the castle of another. And the more I amassed, the more I would covet, until I would even invent accusations against my most faithful subjects in order to have an excuse for obtaining their possessions.

Macduff: This is worse than the former evil. Greed is more deeply rooted in our nature than lust, which soon passes away, and it also has brought monarchs to destruction. Yet that need not prevent you. Your country has wealth and plenty enough to give you all you can desire, even of that which is absolutely your own. These are endurable evils, if you have virtues to counterbalance them.

Malcolm: Nay, I shall disappoint you there also. The virtues which suit a monarch, such as equity, truthfulness, moderation, stability, generosity, steadiness of purpose, compassion, humility, zeal, long-suffering, valor and endurance, I have not the slightest savor of. But I am so skilled in wickedness that I can devise many various ways of committing every evil act. I would even cast out sweet peace and all kindly agreement from this world, overturn the tranquillity of the state and cause the harmony of the world to be overwhelmed in universal strife.

Macduff: O, my unhappy country.

Malcolm: My character is as I have told you. Now, tell me if you think that one such as I have described is worthy to rule any realm.

Macduff: Worthy to rule! Unworthy even to exist. O, wretched people, groaning under the sway of a cruel usurper, when can thou ever hope to see sound and prosperous days once more? The rightful heir of thy crown, thy only hope of deliverance, stands self-accused and self-condemned, slandering by that accusation the noble parentage from which he springs. The king, thy father, was a man of most pure and holy life. Thy royal mother lived a life of daily preparation for death, and spent by far the greater part of her time in prayer and supplication to God. Adieu! Those crimes of which you accuse yourself have pronounced my sentence of exile—it is useless to return to my native land. My heart can now hold nothing but despair!

Malcolm: Noble thane, this outburst of strong feeling, bearing as it does the unmistakable ring of sincerity and truth, has banished the last trace of dark suspicion from my mind, and proved to me thy absolute uprightness and good faith. The wicked tyrant has already, many times, attempted by tricks like these to deceive me into entering Scotland, where he would have me in his power. I have learned to exercise a sober judgment, unless a too-ready belief should hurry me into some act which I should afterward regret. Now, I unhesitatingly put myself into thy hands, and God shall judge between us, if I do not deal truly with thee. And, also, for thy comfort, I now deny all that I have said against myself. I swear to thee that the evil practices of which I accused myself are utterly unknown to me. I have never perjured myself, never sinned against a woman, never coveted the possessions of others—indeed, scarcely cared for what I possessed myself. I have always regarded as sacred my sworn word. And so far from proving treacherous to a friend, I would not play the traitor to the fiend himself, if he trusted me. I love truth and honor as I prize my own existence. This misrepresentation of myself is the first falsehood I have uttered. What I really am, in truth and in deed, belongs wholly to thee and to my poor country, to be used entirely for her service. Indeed, the old earl of Northumbria was already prepared to set out with a large force, before thy arrival. Now, we can accompany him, and may the fortune of our enterprise end as happily as this difference of ours, justifying itself by its result! Why do you say nothing?

Macduff: When such unpleasing assertions are followed so quickly by such glad news, it is difficult, at first, to make them agree.

[Enter a doctor.]

Malcolm: Well, we will speak of this again, presently. Does King Edward propose leaving the palace, sir?

Doctor: Yes, my good lord. A number of poor creatures are awaiting his arrival to cure them. The disease with which they are afflicted is too strong for the best attempts of the healing art, but God has given the holy king such a wonderful power, that they recover immediately after he has touched them.

Malcolm: My thanks to you, sir.

[Exit doctor.]

Macduff: What malady does he speak of?

Malcolm: It is named the "king's evil." During my stay in this country, I have frequently seen the saintly monarch perform this wonderful cure. Only he can tell, with what prayers and entreaties he prevails. But it is true that he restores to health many unfortunate creatures afflicted with strange and unsightly diseases, looked upon as absolutely hopeless by the physicians. He gives to each one a stamped coin, which they suspend around their necks, and prayers are offered during the ceremony. It is said that he bequeaths this wonderful gift of healing to his heirs, and also that he is endowed with the ability to predict the future. Many other heavenly benefits surround him, proclaiming the saintliness of his life.

[*Enter Ross.*]

Macduff: Who is this approaching?

Malcolm: It is a Scotsman, yet I am unacquainted with him.

Macduff: My dear kinsman, gladly do I see thee here.

Malcolm: Now I recognize him. O kindly heaven, may the reason that keeps me a stranger to my own land and to the faces of my own countrymen be speedily removed!

Ross: Heartily do I wish that may be so, my lord.

Malcolm: Is our poor country yet in existence?

Ross: Poor miserable land! It scarcely dares to feel that it still lives. No longer can we call it our parent, it has become a tomb, a sepulcher. All faces in that land show care and sorrow, except only those too ignorant to understand their country's plight. Sounds of despair and grief are uttered, without any taking heed or note of them. Continued suffering has made men callous and indifferent. Intense and extreme distress has become an ordinary commonplace condition of mind. The tolling of the death bell scarcely excites sufficient interest to make people inquire as to who is the latest victim, and the lives of innocent and unoffending people are cut off suddenly, before even the blossom they placed in their bonnet has had time to wither. Before sickness even attacks them, we hear they are dead.

Macduff: O, sorrowful tale, so minutely detailed, and yet so accurate!

Malcolm: What is the latest misfortune?

Ross: Every moment pours out a new tale of woe. If we tell what happened an hour ago, we are laughed at, as bringers of stale news.

Macduff: How fares Lady Macduff?

Ross: She is well.

Macduff: And my little ones?

Ross: The same.

Macduff: The villainous Macbeth has not disturbed them?

Ross: They were resting undisturbed when I was there.

Macduff: Come, cousin, do not be so hesitant with your words. Let us know all.

Ross: When I left Scotland to bring you the news I have carried with so heavy a heart, it was being currently reported that numbers of good men were taking the field of battle, and I believed this readily, because I saw Macbeth's forces being gathered together. If only you would come to Scotland now. This is the most favorable occasion. Your very presence there would bring every man to your side, and make even the women join in the struggle to free themselves from their overwhelming miseries.

Malcolm: Let them take courage. We are coming to their deliverance. The generous King Edward has allowed us a large force, and the valiant Siward will lead them. There is no more skilful and experienced a soldier to be found in all Christendom.

Ross: O, that I also could give you consolation and hope, as your words give to us! But the tale I have to tell should be cried out to the desolate wilderness, where the sound could be caught by no human ear.

Macduff: Does thy tale relate to the common grief of the land, or to some private sorrow, concerning one person alone?

Ross: All right-minded people share in this sorrow, but it chiefly concerns yourself, noble thane.

Macduff: Tell me, tell me quickly. If it concerns me, keep me not in suspense.

Ross: Do not hate me forever, because I have to acquaint you with the most terrible grief you have ever known.

Macduff: Ah! My heart forebodes what you have to say!

Ross: Your mansion was suddenly attacked, and all that were in it, inhumanly slain. If I were to describe how it was done, the recital would only add your death to the slaughter.

Malcolm: O gracious powers! Nay, my lord, do not turn away and conceal your face so sadly. Let your grief speak. The woe that is endured in silence often proves too heavy for the overladen heart.

Macduff: My little ones slain, did you say?

Ross: Your little ones, their mother and your followers: every person the castle contained.

Macduff: And I not there! And my wife?

Ross: Even so.

Malcolm: Take comfort, and let our woes be cured by the terrible vengeance we shall take for them.

Macduff: Talk not to me of "comfort" and of "cure." You have no children. What can you understand? O, fiend! Every single one? Did you say every one of my sweet babes and their mother, at one deadly stroke?

Malcolm: I beg you, contend with your sorrow bravely.

Macduff: I shall conquer it presently but, just now, I can only feel it most humanly. All I can think of is that I had children and a wife who were most dear to me—now I have none.

O, could the powers above see their dire peril, and never intervene to save them! And it was on my account! It was for me, worthless creature that I am, that they were slain. For no offences of their own, but because of the hatred the tyrant bears to me. God give them peace!

Malcolm: Let the intensity of your sorrow give similar strength to your rage, and sharpen your blade to do its part. Let it not dull your heart with pain, but lend it force and fury.

Macduff: O, I could yield to feminine weakness and weep, and my tongue could utter wild boasts of vengeance! Please, kind heaven, hinder us not. Let us quickly reach our enemies, and let me meet this devil face to face. If he succeeds in escaping from me, when once he is within reach of my sword-arm, then may heaven pardon him his atrocious crimes!

Malcolm: These words have the right ring to them! Let us hurry to King Edward, for the troops are all in readiness, and all we need now is to pay our farewells to the king. The tyrant's power is tottering to its fall, and heaven now sends us to be the instruments of vengeance. Take comfort from that thought. Let the darkness prevail ever so long, light will come at last.

[Exit.]

ACT V · SCENE 1

[*Dunsinane. An anteroom in the castle.*]

[*Enter a doctor and a waiting gentlewoman.*]

Doctor: We have remained on guard together for two nights, and I have seen nothing to confirm what you told me. When did you last see her walk in her sleep?

Gentlewoman: Since the king went to war, she has, several times, risen from her couch, put on her dressing gown and then opened her cabinet and taken out paper, upon which, after having doubled it, she wrote something. After reading over what she had written, she fastened it up securely and then returned to her couch. She was in a deep slumber the whole time.

Doctor: It is a great disturbance of the usual course of nature for one to perform the acts of a waking person while the body is, at the same time, resting in sleep. Have you ever heard her say anything, in addition to seeing her walking about and performing various acts, in this disturbance of her mind during sleep?

Gentlewoman: I have heard her say things which I shall never repeat.

Doctor: You may safely repeat them to me. And, indeed, it is most appropriate that I should be told.

Gentlewoman: The assertion would only rest upon my bare word, as no one else has ever heard her. So I shall not repeat them to anyone.

[*Enter Lady Macbeth with a candle.*]

See, she is coming! This is the way she always looks, and, look, she is in a sound sleep. Conceal yourself, and watch carefully.

Doctor: How did she get that candle?

Gentlewoman: It was in her room. By her explicit wish, she is never without a light.

Doctor: Her eyes are not closed.

Gentlewoman: No, but there is no intelligence in them. They see nothing.

Doctor: What is she doing? See how she is rubbing her hands.

Gentlewoman: She does that continually. I have seen her rub her hands in that manner, as though she were washing them, for many minutes together.

Lady Macbeth: Here is a mark still.

Doctor: Listen! She begins to talk. I will note down her words to ensure that I remember them correctly.

Lady Macbeth: Get thee gone, accursed stain! Disappear, I insist! Hark! The clock strikes! It is the hour. Now it must be done. 'Tis dismal in hell! For shame, sir! You a warrior, and terrified by your deed! Why should we be afraid, even if it comes to light? None can challenge us to answer for it. But one would never have thought he would bleed so much.

Doctor: Do you note what she says?

Lady Macbeth: Macduff had a wife. What has become of her? O, I shall never get these hands clean! Cease those starts, my lord. Stop, you spoil everything.

Doctor: Shame on you, madam. You know what should never have been known.

Gentlewoman: She has said what should never have been uttered, I am certain. None can tell what secret knowledge she has.

Lady Macbeth: It smells of blood even yet. All the fragrant spices of the East are not sufficient to purify this one tiny hand. Woe! Alas!

Doctor: How deep a sigh she utters! It is a heavily burdened heart that sends it forth.

Gentlewoman: I would not have such a sorrow-laden heart in my breast even for all the royal rank of the poor lady.

Doctor: Well, well, well—

Gentlewoman: I hope it may be well, doctor.

Doctor: I cannot hope to cure this malady, it is beyond my powers. Still, it is not unusual for those who have been addicted to this habit to die peacefully in their beds at the last.

Lady Macbeth: Bathe your hands. Get your gown on. Do not look so white and terrified. Once more I say, Banquo is in his grave. He cannot rise out of it.

Doctor: Ah! Is it thus?

Lady Macbeth: To our room, to rest. Someone knocks to be admitted. Come, come, let me lead you. It is done now, and cannot be helped. Come, to bed, to bed, to bed!

[*Exit.*]

Doctor: Will she now go to lie down?

Gentlewoman: Yes, at once.

Doctor: There are many evil reports circulating, and minds overcharged with guilty secrets and troubles will make them known, if only to the senseless pillows on which they rest. Strange and terrible deeds bring a similar retribution. This poor lady is more in need of the treatments of holy men than those of a doctor of medicine. Heaven be merciful to us all! Take care of her. Leave nothing near her with which she might do herself harm, and watch her continually. There, good night now. She has almost stupefied my mind, and shown to my eyes something which has utterly astounded me. My thoughts are busy, but I cannot give them words.

Gentlewoman: Good night, kind sir.

[*Exit.*]

ACT V · SCENE 2
[*The country near Dunsinane.*]
[*Drums and flags. Enter Menteith, Caithness, Angus, Lennox and soldiers.*]

Menteith: The English force is close at hand. The leaders are young Malcolm, the earl of Northumbria and the noble thane of Fife. They are eager for revenge. Indeed, the injuries that touch them so nearly would cause even a dead man to rise and come to take part in the fierce and bloody struggle.

Angus: They are coming in the direction of Birnam Wood, and we shall join them not far from it.

Caithness: Is it known whether Malcolm's younger. brother is with him?

Lennox: No, my lord, he is not with Malcolm, for I have a list of all the nobles in his company. But young Siward is there, and many other beardless boys, now for the first time displaying their manhood in action.

Menteith: What is Macbeth doing?

Caithness: He has greatly strengthened his castle of Dunsinane. His enemies report that he is insane, but those who do not go to that extreme of animosity against him say he is merely possessed by a martial rage. But, certainly, he is unable to keep either himself or his disloyal party under command.

Angus: He is now reaping the reward of his former assassinations. They clog his movements and he cannot shake off their effects. Every moment he hears of some new desertion from his party, which reminds him that he first showed the example of treachery. Even those who still remain under his command only obey him from a sense of duty, and give him no support in loyalty or affection. His position and state are ready to fall from him like an ill-fitting garment, not made for the wearer.

Menteith: We cannot then wonder that his harassed brain is ready to give way, when he must feel that his whole position is a false one.

Caithness: Well, let us set forth, and give our loyal service to that prince who has a rightful claim upon it. Let us join him, who will be the cure for all the ills we suffer from in our disordered commonwealth, and mingle all our powers, nay, our lifeblood, if necessary, with that healing solution.

Lennox: We will freely give whatever is required to cause the royal remedy to flourish, and bring the destructive upstart to ruin. Forward. To Birnam Wood.

[Exit, marching.]

ACT V · SCENE 3

[Dunsinane. A room in the castle.]
[Enter Macbeth, doctor and attendants.]

Macbeth: Tell me no further news. They may all desert me if they will. I care not. Fear cannot infect my spirit until the forest moves from Birnam to Dunsinane. What is there in young Malcolm to frighten me? He was born of woman, therefore he has no power against me. The weird sisters, to whom is given the knowledge of future events, solemnly declared I do not need to fear human enemies, for no man who is born of woman can prevail against me. Then let the traitors desert, and join the forces of the Saxon gluttons. The spirit that directs me shall never droop with dread, nor terror have any power to move my heart.

[Enter a servant.]

A curse upon thy white face, fellow! What has given thee that terrified look?

Servant: An immense number of—

Macbeth: Geese, knave?

Servant: Troops, my lord.

Macbeth: Begone, and get some color into thy face! Prick it until blood covers it, if thou cannot get it otherwise, and see that thou hide its whiteness, thou faint-hearted fellow. What troops are they, clown? Curse thee, that bleached face of thine is enough, of itself, to suggest terror. What troops, frightened one?

Servant: May it please Your Highness, the enemy's troops.

Macbeth: Away with those cheeks! [*Exit servant.*] Seyton! It fills me with despair to see—Seyton, hearest thou? Now it has come to the point. This conflict will decide whether I am to be happily victorious once and for all, or be deposed without more delay. I do not greatly care to live longer. I have reached the autumn of my days, when the powers begin to fail and flag. I cannot even hope to possess those compensations which are usually granted to the decline of life, such as affection and respect, willing service and many loving companions. In place of these, I must expect the fervent, if subdued, hatred of my countrymen, the outward respect which goes no farther than the lips, mere words of service, with no heart behind them. Even my wretched followers would like to refuse, except that fear forbids them. Seyton!

[*Enter Seyton.*]

Seyton: What does Your Majesty desire?

Macbeth: Is there any news?

Seyton: Only confirmation of our former news, Your Highness.

Macbeth: I will never surrender, though my body be cut in pieces. Bring me my harness.

Seyton: You need not arm yourself yet, sir.

Macbeth: Nevertheless, I will be ready. Let more men ride throughout the district, and put to death any whom they find discouraging their fellows. What is your patient like, doctor?

Doctor: She has no bodily ailment, Your Highness. But her brain is disturbed and harassed by an endless succession of wild imaginations and ideas, which effectively prevent her gaining any benefit from her sleep.

Macbeth: That must be remedied. With all thy skill, can thou do nothing to ease the tortured soul; to banish wholly from the sad remembrance deep and abiding grief; and, from the brain, to erase the woes that are written there; and, with some grateful remedy, to cause forgetfulness of those so-heavy sorrows and, thus, relieve the overladen heart of that which so oppresses it?

Doctor: None can aid the patient there. He must be his own physician.

Macbeth: Then fling away your remedies, for they are worthless. Never will I seek their aid. Come, dress me with my armor and hand me my baton. Send those men as I told you, Seyton. I am deserted by my peasants, doctor—now, fellow, be quick! Doctor, if thou could only make a medical analysis of the condition of this country, discover its complaint and name the remedy that would restore it to its former healthy and wholesome condition, I would sing thy praises until the earth would echo with them, and repeat thy fame. Take that off again. Can thou find some medicine or potion to clear these southerners out of the land? Thou hast heard of their approach?

Doctor: Yes, my liege. Your Majesty's arrangements to meet them let us know that they are near.

Macbeth: Carry that out with me. The near approach of ruin and destruction shall never cause me to fear, until Birnam Wood marches against me to this hill.

Doctor: [*Aside.*] If I were safely out of this castle, no considerations of gain would ever tempt me to re-enter it.

[*Exit.*]

ACT V · SCENE 4

[*Country near Birnam Wood.*]
[*Drums and flags. Enter Malcolm, old Siward and his son, Macduff, Menteith, Caithness, Angus, Lennox, Ross and soldiers, marching.*]

Malcolm: I am hopeful, friends and kinsmen, that soon we shall be able to live at peace in our homes, without the fear of secret spies and assassinations.

Menteith: We are assured of it.

Siward: What forest is this we have reached?

Menteith: It is called Birnam Wood.

Malcolm: Soldiers, each of you cut down a branch from the trees, and carry it in front of you as we march. By this means, we shall conceal the strength of our force and deceive the spies of Macbeth.

Soldiers: We obey, my lord.

Siward: It is still reported that Macbeth remains secure in his strong castle, willing to sustain a siege.

Malcolm: His chief confidence is placed in the strength of Dunsinane, for his followers are all leaving him, wherever they can see a favorable opportunity. Many have renounced their allegiance, and he has none to serve him now but those who are obliged to do so, and they do it with an unwilling mind.

Macduff: Let us wait until the issue is decided, when we shall be able to give a correct opinion. Meantime, it is our business to be diligent in our martial duties.

Siward: We shall soon have an opportunity to decide whether we are to gain or lose. It is all very well to conjecture beforehand, but nothing is certain yet. Battle must finally decide the result, so forward with our army.

[Exit, marching.]

ACT V · SCENE 5

[Dunsinane. Inside the castle.]
[Enter Macbeth, Seyton and soldiers, with drums and flags.]

Macbeth: Let our flags be displayed on the battlements, and wave defiance to the enemy's army, for they advance in ever-increasing numbers. But Dunsinane's walls are strong. They will find it impossible to take the castle by assault, and they are welcome to camp before it until they are destroyed by hunger and fever. Had they not been strengthened and reinforced by so many who should have fought on our side, we would have fearlessly given them battle face to face on the plain, and driven them to return from where they came. [*A cry of women, within.*] What are those cries?

Seyton: The wails of women, my liege.

[Exit.]

Macbeth: I scarcely know, now, what it is to feel any dread. I have known the days when my whole being would freeze with horror on hearing a scream in the night. And the hairs of my head would move and rise, as if alive, at a tale of terror. Now nothing can frighten me. I have for so long been intimately concerned with hideous thoughts and gruesome deeds that the most appalling sights and sounds have lost their power to affect me.

[Re-enter Seyton.]

What was the reason for those cries?

Seyton: My liege, they wailed for the queen, who has just died.

Macbeth: That should have happened later. We would then have had time to attend to such news. Thus it is, that day after day, and night after night crawls slowly by, and we look forward to each tomorrow, hoping it will be better than today, but it merely drags on and on, and will do so to the very end of the ages. And every slow day that passes shows more foolish wretches the path down to their earthy grave. Fail and die, thou momentary gleam of the lamp of life! We would be happier were thy flame quenched earlier.

This existence of ours is a mere unreal image in a fleeting show. It is like an actor who occupies the stage for a time, playing his part with pompous dignity and an artificial and simulated passion. Then, when his brief part is over, he vanishes, and is immediately forgotten. It is like a story in the mouth of a brainless fool, sounding important and noisy enough but, in the end, found to be utterly meaningless.

[Enter a messenger.]

Well, thou art here to say something. Say it at once.

Messenger: Most noble king, I have seen a sight which I ought to tell you of, but I know not how to put it into words.

Macbeth: Come, tell it!

Messenger: I was sentinel upon the rising ground of Dunsinane, and was looking in the direction of Birnam, when, presently, I thought I saw the whole forest move from its place.

Macbeth: Thou lying villain!

Messenger: It is true, my lord. I will abide your displeasure if I have spoken falsely. You may see it advancing, a walking forest, over the whole intervening distance to the castle.

Macbeth: If thou hast brought me lies, I will suspend thee from the first tree within reach, until thou dry up and waste away with starvation. But, if thy tale be true, I would as willingly endure that fate myself, as believe what this foretells!

My strength gives way at the tidings. The evil ones have played with me, deceiving me with falsehoods that are partial truths. They promised me safety until Birnam Wood should move from its place, a thing not naturally possible. Now, it seems the impossibility has come to pass.

To arms! Turn out and meet the foe! If this be true, which he swears, it is useless either to remain within the walls, or to try to escape. I am sick at heart with life. I wish that this were now the end of this miserable world. Sound the alarm! Now storm, destruction and ruin, do your worst! Retreat and escape are both hopeless, but we can at least seek a warrior's death!

[Exit.]

ACT V · SCENE 6

[Dunsinane. In front of the castle.]
[Drums and flags. Enter Malcolm, old Siward, Macduff and their army, with branches of trees.]

Malcolm: We have advanced far enough now. Discard the leafy shelters that have hidden your numbers, and reveal yourselves in your full strength. Noble earl, you and your valiant son shall have command of the first division to advance. We and the brave thane of Fife will command the rest, and do whatever is necessary to support you.

Siward: Adieu, sirs. If we meet Macbeth's forces this night, we will show whether we can contend against him worthily. If we cannot, may we be vanquished ourselves!

Macduff: Give orders that all the bugles be blown—those loud-voiced heralds of wounds and deadly destruction. Let them all be sounded.

[Exit.]

ACT V · SCENE 7

[Another part of the field.]
[Sounds of battle. Enter Macbeth.]

Macbeth: I am hedged in and surrounded here. They have me firmly, and I must fight until the performance is over, like a tormented bear. Where is the man who was not born of woman? He is the only one I am to dread.

[Enter young Siward.]

Young Siward: Who art thou?

Macbeth: It would strike thee with terror, were I to say.

Young Siward: Never, even though thy name were more terrible than any fiend of hell.

Macbeth: I am Macbeth.

Young Siward: Not even Satan could have given a name that I hate so deeply.

Macbeth: Or dread more deeply.

Young Siward: This is false, detestable oppressor, and I will prove it with my weapon upon thee.

[They fight, and young Siward is slain.]

Macbeth: Thy valor is useless. Thou could not vanquish me. No blade may harm me, used by one who was born of woman. I mock at them all.

[Exit.]
[Sounds of battle. Enter Macduff.]

Macduff: The tumult rises in that direction. Villainous tyrant, let me behold thee! If any arm except mine deal thy death-blow, I shall never be freed from the reproachful faces of my dear ones. Thy poor miserable followers, who bear arms for their living, I cannot attack. If I find thee not, my blade must return to its scabbard unused, with its great task unaccomplished. That uproar indicates thy presence—some notable one fights there. Kind fate, bring us face to face, and I desire no more.

[Exit. Sounds of battle.]
[Enter Malcolm and old Siward.]

Siward: Come in this direction, prince. The castle has been given up without a struggle. Macbeth's followers are fighting both for and against him, and your Scottish lords bear themselves gallantly. Little remains now to be done. The battle is almost over, and your troops are on the point of victory.

Malcolm: Many of our opponents intentionally aimed their blows aside, and did not attempt to kill us.

Siward: My lord, advance and take possession of the tyrant's fortress.

[Exit. Sounds of battle.]

ACT V · SCENE 8

[Another part of the field.]
[Enter Macbeth.]

Macbeth: I will not imitate the example of the foolish Romans, and turn my weapon upon myself when the day is lost. As long as I see any foes living, I prefer to use it against them.

Macduff: Turn! Face me, thou fiend of hell!

Macbeth: I have shunned thee, and thee alone, this day. Begone! I have the guilt of too many of thy house already upon me. I would not want to add another.

Macduff: I come not to argue, but to fight. My blade shall speak for me, thou hateful wretch, more evil than words can say!

[They fight.]

Macbeth: Thy efforts are in vain, thou cannot harm me. As soon might thou make an impression on the air, which cannot feel thy weapon, as inflict any wound on me. Go, combat with foes who may be vanquished. I may not. My life is protected by a spell. I am invulnerable to the blade of any man who was born of woman.

Macduff: Then thy spell is useless. Give up thy hopes of safety. Ask the evil spirit, whose servant thou art, and learn that Macduff was not, in the accepted sense, born of woman.

Macbeth: Curses on thee for saying that! It shakes my courage and almost makes me fear. Let none ever trust those deceiving spirits that lie and quibble with words of double meaning, that fulfil the letter and mere sound of the words, but ruin our hopes, which were founded on the meaning and spirit of them. I refuse the combat.

Macduff: Coward! Surrender, then, and we will spare thy life, that thou may be an example and exhibit to all the world. We will exhibit thee to the crowd, as curious animals are, with sign and inscription, "Come, and behold the oppressor!"

Macbeth: Never will I surrender to submit myself to the boyish son of Duncan, and to be hooted at by all the vulgar crowd. Though the false promises have been broken, though the imagined security they gave is proven a mere deception, I will yet attempt the struggle, and dare thee to the end. With my strong shield before me, I challenge thee to renew the fight, and cursed be the one who shall first show signs of yielding.

[Exit fighting. Sounds of battle.]
[Retreat. Flourish of trumpets. Enter, with drum and colors, Malcolm, old Siward, Ross, the other thanes and soldiers.]

Malcolm: I wish that all our company were now safely gathered here.

Siward: In a struggle like this we cannot expect all to escape uninjured. Some few cannot but be killed. By the number of our friends whom I see around me, this remarkable victory appears to have been gained with little loss to our side.

Malcolm: The valiant young Siward and the thane of Fife are still absent.

Ross: Young Siward has fulfilled his duty as a warrior, brave earl, and has met with a warrior's end. He lived long enough to prove himself no mere boy, but a manly soldier, fighting valiantly, yielding no foot of ground to the foe. And, when he had thus shown his worth, he fell.

Siward: He is killed, then?

Ross: Yes, and his body has been carried from the battlefield. Your grief will be great. But, if it should be calculated according to his merit, then you must mourn forever, for that was immeasurable.

Siward: Were his wounds in front?

Ross: Yes, every one received facing the foe.

Siward: Then let us leave him in God's keeping. He has died well. Even if I had an unnumbered family of sons, I could not desire to see them end their lives in a nobler way. So farewell, Siward, thy end has come.

Malcolm: I will mourn him longer, for he merits our loving grief.

Siward: That will suffice. He has fulfilled his duty, discharged his task and died bravely. There is no more to say. God keep him! I see better consolation approaching.

[Re-enter Macduff, with Macbeth's head.]

Macduff: Greeting, King Malcolm of Scotland! Such is now thy title. See, I bring thee the head of the tyrant who defrauded thee of thy throne and kingdom. Now we can breathe in a free and wholesome age, no longer prevented by oppression. Thou art surrounded, at this moment, by the flowers of all thy realm. They echo my greeting in their hearts. Now I desire them to acclaim thee with their tongues. God save the king of Scotland!

All: God save the king of Scotland!

[Flourish of trumpets.]

Malcolm: It shall not be long before we repay the loving, loyal aid which all have rendered to us. And here we bestow upon each of you the title of earl, my faithful citizens and friends, the first bearers of that high rank in Scotland. There are many things suitable for the commencement of a new and better era, which shall, in due course, have our attention. We shall recall our acquaintances and friends from the foreign shores where they sought refuge from the dangers that menaced their lives under the oppressor's rule. We shall bring to justice those who were the servants and instruments of his villainy, and that of his wicked wife, who, we understand, has taken her own life. These things shall first be done. And, afterward, whatever else is necessary for our country's health, shall by God's help be performed in just and suitable degree, as time and opportunity offer. Accept our heartfelt gratitude to each and all, and our cordial invitation to the ceremony of our coronation, which will take place at Scone.

[Flourish of trumpets. Exit.]

NOTES